MW01567775

Amy -

Break some Rules!

Monica

Your Face Isn't Finished Until Your Lipstick Is On

Rule of the Women's Success Game

By
Monica Cornetti

Your Face Isn't Finished Until Your Lipstick Is On

Rule of the Women's Success Game

By
Monica Cornetti

EntrepreNow! Press
Little Elm, TX

Your Face Isn't Finished Until Your Lipstick is On
First Edition
Copyright © 2011 by Monica Cornetti

Published by EntrepreNow! Press
2765 E. Eldorado Pkwy, Suite #215-123
Little Elm, TX 75068

All rights reserved. This book may not be used or reproduced in any manner, in whole or in part, stored in a retrieval system or transmitted in any form (by electronic, mechanical, photocopied, recorded or other means) without written permission from the author, except as permitted by United States copyright law.

No liability is assumed with respect to the use of information contained herein. While every precaution has been taken in the preparation of this book, the author assumes no responsibility for errors or omissions. Neither is any liability assumed for damages resulting from the use of information contained herein.

Cover art by Azure Marketing
www.azuremarcom.com

Editing and layout by Circumference Communications
www.CircumferenceCommunications.com

ISBN: 978-0-9789229-1-7

Printed in the United States of America

Acknowledgements

Thanks to all the bright, energetic, self-sacrificing, awesome women in my life who, time after time, have helped me become a better person. You know who you are, even if I didn't mention you by name in this book. Your willingness to bend the rules—and break them when necessary—is a source of validation and motivation to me.

Thanks to my editor, Jonathan Peters, Ph.D., who is a steady source of information and support. Every step of the way you have been there to listen to my doubts, answer my questions, and point me back to center whenever I get lost.

Thanks to my creative consultant, Elyse Erickson. It's amazing how much creativity can take place over a bottle of wine and block of cheese. You are a continuous source of inspiration and encouragement to me.

Thanks to my mom who taught me, "Life doesn't come to you … you have to go find it." At the time those were words I didn't want to hear, but they have proven to be a foundation to live by in my adult life.

Thanks to my sister, Melanie, the source of so many great stories for my seminars and speaking engagements. Although we are as different as two people can be, our hearts are knit together with a bond of sisterly love that cannot be broken.

And finally, to my husband, Mark, who, at the age of 21, had no idea what the words, "for better or for worse" really meant, you are the gentle force that holds us together. Thank you for bending and not breaking. I love you.

Dedication

This book is dedicated to my three sons, Lou, Nick and Joe, whom I love more than ordinary words on a page can express.

Their encouragement, love, and never-ending questioning of the rules have proven to be a steady force to shape me into the woman I am today. In spite of my many mistakes, they have grown to be awesome young men who daily light up the lives of the people around them.

Of all the professional titles I proudly answer to, such as "international speaker" and "world class instructor," I am still delighted to be called simply – *MOM*.

Table of Contents

Introduction 1

Chapter 1:
    Your Face Isn't Finished 9

Chapter 2:
    The Rules, They Are Always There . 23

Chapter 3:
    Reframe Your Worth 33

Chapter 4:
    Let Your Heart be Your GPS 47

Chapter 5:
    A Little Courage Goes a Long Way . 59

Chapter 6:
    Refuse to Listen to the Chatter 73

Chapter 7:
    Change the Script 85

Chapter 8:
    God Colored Outside the Lines:
    So Can You 95

Chapter 9:
    The World Needs You! 109

Chapter 10:
    Be Lovingly Consistent 121

Conclusion 133

Introduction

In 2002, my life was in shambles. The career I had given ten years of my life to was over. It was not a career I had even wanted, but when it ended, I was so devastated that I sat in a dark room and cried for days.

Things were over because of bad moral and ethical choices I had made. And, because the organization I had been working for could have been badly tarnished by my actions, I felt I needed to resign.

For ten years I had given this career and organization a consistent 60 plus hours every week. I took my computer with me on all of our vacations, even during the seven years before I had a laptop. My phone rang at all times of the day and night, and I was expected to take all calls. My commitment to the mission and vision of the organization was real, yet at the same time, there was definitely something wrong.

I had always wanted to be the kind of mom who was very involved with her children and their activities, but the nature of the job prevented me from being deeply involved in their lives. I often missed their games and music gigs. Because of the long work hours and pressure of the job, I was rarely present, even when I was at home.

Inside, I knew I wasn't the right fit for the job, or the organization. I worked so hard because I was too cowardly to stand up to the influential people who told me I was supposed to be in that position and work as hard as I did.

To escape from the constant pressure, I planned short trips to nearby Houston or Rockport with my boys. I know now that I was trying to make space for myself as a distinct person, but changing a physical location wasn't going to solve the real problems.

I told my closest friends, "I'm becoming a shell of my former self. I'm afraid if I stay much longer, I won't recognize me anymore." I had migrated to a place where I neither appreciated my abilities, nor trusted my instincts.

What I didn't know at the time was that just because you haven't done something doesn't mean you can't. You can learn anything if you surround yourself with experts who know how to do what it is you want to accomplish. I've learned now not to ignore the triggers of anxiety or constant discomfort. You have to pay attention to low-grade dissatisfaction before it turns into potential self-destruction.

I wasn't strong or courageous enough to proactively resign from my position. Instead, I put myself into a position where I had no other choice. The result was my friends and colleagues had to protect themselves from any association with me. I became someone they could not, or should not, associate with. The feeling of abandonment was so overwhelming that I didn't know how I was going to make it.

At the time, I was in the habit of running three to five miles in the evenings. As I ran, the pressure in my chest was so intense that I would think, "I am going to have a heart attack right here and die." I would slow my stride, walk for a few steps and then think, "Oh my god ... what if I don't die right here, right now?"

What saved me is that I'm the type of person who never took failure lightly. I knew I had to get some kind of forward motion, or my family and I were going to be in real trouble.

After a few false starts, I started consulting with local business associates, helping them with their business and marketing plans. These people gave me an opportunity to use my skills and expertise, and made it possible to get my focus going in a positive direction. They helped me by allowing me to help them.

From the consulting efforts came an invitation to speak at a women's meeting on the topic of "How to Write a Business Plan." Never mind that I had no background in public speaking. My role had always been one of support. In fact, up until that point, I had stayed strictly behind the scenes. I was married to a performer; I was a mother and a business administrator. The thought of speaking in front of people made me so nervous that I thought I would lose my lunch. However, I decided the time had come for me to make a drastic change.

I was so nervous the morning of the event. I didn't know if I could make the presentation. As I stood at the podium, my heart beat out of control. When I looked down, I thought I could actually see the left side of my suit jacket moving in and out.

The audience was a small group of about 20 women, most of whom I knew. The presentation went well, and the participants seemed to enjoy it. I actually gave them information they could use.

And most surprisingly, I liked it.

As I drove home I thought, "I want to do more of that. I wonder how?" I stopped by our local bookstore and picked up a copy of Paul Karasik's book *How to Make it Big in the Seminar Business*.

Introduction

That weekend I poured over the book. I took voracious notes, dog-earring and sticky tabbing countless pages. A fire began growing inside of me. I thought, "I can do this!"

But I ran into countless people who gave me reasons why I would fail ... again. One person told me, "You can't start a new career at 43. Statistics show it takes at least 7-10 years to become an expert in any profession."

Those were fighting words to me. If nothing else, I was going to prove the naysayers wrong. It was time to step out of the box that I had been in for ten years. If there was going to be any chance for me to be a successful business woman, the time was now. I began forging my own path.

Following Karasik's advice, I applied to three of the big public seminar companies. One was unwilling to consider me because they required at least a Master's Degree. The second one admired my credentials, but didn't see a good fit for me. But the third, Fred Pryor/CareerTrack Seminars, called and asked me to attend their three day certification class, to certify with them as a trainer. I was so scared and excited at the same time.

One of the requirements of certification was a three-minute video of me giving a live presentation. That was going to be rather tough to do, since I had given only one presentation and there were no cameras in the room to record it.

So I gathered my few friends, set up chairs, recruited my son Nick to video tape the presentation, and held a seminar on "Time Management Skills" in my living room.

And now, seven years later, I am enjoying the career I always wanted. I have the wonderful opportunity to travel to cities all over the country, and now the world, meeting interesting people as I lead seminars and workshops on a variety of management and leadership topics. Through it all, I have found my passion of helping others move their lives to the next level of success and significance.

I've heard it said, "Success happens to you, and significance happens through you." That is now my motto as I work with people, helping them to achieve their dreams.

So, as my 50th birthday approached, my three boys, who are in their early twenties, decided to shop at a local antique store for my present. I assumed they were looking for a set of crystal rock glasses that I had been hinting at. Instead, they were looking for a book that detailed the life of business women in 1959, the year I was born. Not surprisingly, they did not find one.

What they did find was a 1960 Special Edition of *LIFE* magazine, chronicling the first 25 years of the magazine. Amidst the ads for cigarettes, dog food, hemorrhoid cream and weight loss products (yes, even in 1960) were two articles that featured women. Over 25 years, women got a three-page spread journaling fashion trends, and a second article called "The Abundance of Beauty," a compilation of photographs highlighting truly beautiful women such as Ava Gardner, Audrey Hepburn, Elizabeth Taylor, and Jacqueline Kennedy.

The introduction to the second article discussed how we, as women, outnumbered men, We had more registered voters, and we spent more of the nation's money. The article also listed some of the new careers available to women, such as long-haul trucking, race horse training, and ball club owners. The author stated, "Nothing was sacred anymore, and a few men tried to sound the alarm. But no one tried too hard to put out the fire because ... well, because women, after all, could look the way they do in these pictures."

We look good, so they decided to let us stay and play?

We all know there is a different set of rules for men and women in the game of success. For instance, many people have told me, "If a man had transgressed as you did, he would not have lost his job." And they are probably right. Women are held to different standards than men; therefore, we must find our own paths to success.

There came a time when I felt like it was my responsibility to explore the rules that have had the most impact on my life, and the lives of other women I encounter in my travels.

The rules are different, but when you're smart, you can use them to shape the life that you really want. Don't worry if you are pushing 40, or even 50, and you are still wondering what you want to be when you grow up! It's time to trust yourself, believe in who you are, and learn the rules of the women's success game.

Chapter 1

Your Face Isn't Finished...

"I've never seen a smiling face that was not beautiful."
- Author Unknown

Just to be clear, this is *NOT* a book of beauty tips; however...

As business women, we know that a professional appearance is crucial to our success at work. I've had woman after woman tell me that they had been passed over for a promotion, or had opportunities removed, because of the way they looked. One woman reported that she was told to "Glam it up a little." Another was told, "You should always wear heels and some sort of make-up, even if it's just lipstick."

Looks do matter, and anyone who says otherwise is either placating themselves, or someone they love, or they are simply deceived. Our culture places a high emphasis on looks. Recent studies document that people blessed with good looks earn about 10% more than their average-looking colleagues. They are also more likely to get hired and promoted at work.

To tell women and young girls that they are beautiful just the way they are would undermine the basic proposition of decades of beauty-care advertising. Cosmetic makers have been selling "hope in a jar" since before the time of Cleopatra. These creams and potions promise youth, beauty, sex appeal, and even love for women who use them. It is said Cleopatra's lipsticks were a deep red pigment made from mixing finely crushed beetles and ant's eggs.

Whatever the concoction, one has to ask, "Are we covering up flaws because we feel we have to, or are we attempting to enhance those features we're proud of and want to draw attention to?" Can we enjoy a bright eyeliner, or a sweep of glitter across our brow and cheeks, or does that somehow diminish who we are attempting to be as professional business women. We should be able to choose to wear makeup because it is fun and makes us feel better about ourselves.

It's a fine line that women walk today. It is unbelievable that an attractive woman would be the brightest person on the team, and even more unbelievable if she is a blonde. A woman who is too pretty, whose skirt is too short, shows too much skin, or wears too much makeup, is likely to be judged less promotable than the average looking woman. Of course, when was the last time you saw a male CEO in shorts or a sleeveless shirt. We as business woman have to be smart in our dress and presentation.

For those who are not a "10" on the beauty scale, it may not be a bad idea to glam it up a little. Ultimately, we have to realize our worth, whether or not we could ever grace the cover of *Glamour Magazine*, is not based on our physical beauty. Each of us is special because of who we are. We spend a lot of time seeking validation from other people, and often, spend years trying to be somebody we're not.

It's important to focus on who we are as a total person, and not just what we look like on the outside.

Sizzlin' Sizzle

Think about an achievement that you've had in your life of which you're especially proud. It could be academic, athletic, artistic, emotional, or a major dare you took, anything at all, that when you think about it, it gives you a rewarding feeling.

Now think about what personal traits it took for you to attain that achievement. Was it courage, tenacity, faith, determination, daring, confidence, conviction, willingness to sacrifice? Perhaps it was a network of people, strong family ties, or loyal friendships.

The traits you identify are what I call your "sizzle." They are what make you unique and what draws people to you.

Your friends, family, and co-workers are counting on you to bring your sizzle into every situation. So don't leave home without it.

I do an activity in my seminars to help participants identify their sizzle. In class, I ask each person to draw a picture of the achievement of which they feel most proud. After a few minutes, I have them write on the borders of their pictures all the personal qualities they needed to bring about that achievement.

When finished, I ask the participants to discuss their individual achievements and qualities with their team. I call the activity Bragfest.

When was the last time someone asked you to brag on yourself? Most people find it difficult to brag about their achievements, but team members often break out into cheers, tears, and applause as they share their amazing accomplishments with each other.

It is easy to feel boastful doing an activity like this, but these are all real life characteristics that we need to identify in ourselves to achieve difficult goals. The next time you're feeling insecure or are not quite measuring up, go ahead and conduct your own Bragfest. You'll feel better instantly. Remind yourself that the strengths that helped you accomplish things in the past are going to help you now and in the future.

You got Sizzle baby!

Looks Matter

So, we should take care of ourselves, and acknowledge that looks do matter, but not so much that we forget who we are. Makeup should be something we choose to wear, not something we need to wear, and definitely not something we have to wear. We can blend our internal and external selves to create the very best us to present to the world.

For instance, I've been on a diet since I was three years old, and I am very much aware how I look compared to other women around me.

A few years ago, I lead a seminar in Monterrey, California. I got tremendous reviews from everyone in the room, except one. She was a top level executive in a large cosmetic company, who brought her entire team to the seminar. At every break, she talked with me about ideas that she could implement with her employees following the training. She was excited about getting techniques and tools that would help her take her team to a higher level.

A day of training like that is extremely fulfilling for a presenter. We feel like the hours of preparation and travel have paid off, and that we are truly making a difference in the lives of people.

I was on this euphoric high at the end of the seminar, until I read my evaluations.

The woman, who happened to be around 5'10" and thin, didn't write a single comment about what she learned in the class or how she planned to apply all that I had suggested. Instead, she wrote, "Monica, I would have felt you were more credible from the beginning of the day if you had been wearing a tailored suit and higher heels. I realized once you started teaching that you have knowledge and experience, but at first I wasn't excited about listening to what you had to say. You should really work on losing about 20 pounds."

After reading that, I sat for about 10 minutes, unable to move. All the joy and enthusiasm I had been feeling was destroyed. I couldn't believe she had written those comments. I had gone to school for 20 plus years, worked hard to gain skills and acquire knowledge, was recognized as one of the top five trainers in the company I was contracting with, and all she had to comment on was my clothes and my weight? It still brings tears to my eyes as I write this many years later.

The reality is my career choice puts me on a platform where people are evaluating my worth not so much by what I say, but by how I look.

The Rules Are Different

Let's not deceive ourselves by thinking the rules are the same for women and men. Women are taught to experience themselves in terms of how they look to other women and men. Men are taught to experience themselves in terms of what they can do, such as hit balls, lift things, run and jump, win battles, etc.

I heard a friend discussing her golf score recently and she said, "If you ask a woman why she missed a putt, she's likely to tell you it's because she didn't practice enough. If you ask a man, he is more likely to blame the wind, the cut of the green, or his putter."

Women tend to hold themselves responsible for their discomfort, while men often look outside themselves when they are uncomfortable in a situation.

Despite our increasingly dominant numbers in the workplace, there is no "old girls network" in place to help us pull each other up to the next level. It's time to firmly establish that we will value ourselves and each other based on who we are, not what we look like. Our differences can be cherished, rather than cursed.

Diva Rules

My sister-in-law, Marianne Cornetti, is considered by many to be the world's best Dramatic Verdi Mezzo Soprano. Marianne will tell you that it was what her mom taught her about the rules of the game early in life that has contributed to her world renowned recognition. Her mother, Pat, said, "If you can see your dream, and you believe your dream, you'll achieve it." At the same time, Pat taught Marianne that she had to fight for what she wanted.

Marianne grew up with two older brothers and no other girls in the neighborhood. She had no one to play with except the boys—and the boys didn't want to play with a girl.

Whenever there was a pick-up baseball game, Marianne would run home crying and say, "They won't let me play!"

Her mom's response would be, "You have to make them let you play." When Marianne insisted they wouldn't, Pat would reply, "Figure out a way. Go out and make them let you play."

One afternoon, in a state of complete frustration, Marianne finally figured out a strategy that would work. She walked onto the ball field and lay down on the ground between the pitcher's mound and home plate. She knew that if the boys hit her with the ball they would be in big trouble.

The boys finally gave in and put her in the outfield. At first the balls would land all around her, and she even got hit in the head a couple times. Eventually, she learned how to play and became quite good. Soon the boys came knocking at her door to ask if she would play second base for them.

Even at places like the Metropolitan Opera House, Marianne had to figure out how to make them let her into the game. She learned that if you do small roles, you'll do them forever. She felt like she was back in the outfield waiting for the big roles to be hit to her.

In 1998, she said good-bye to the Met when she told them, "No more small roles." She also told them she'd be back when she had big roles.

Sure enough, four years later she performed again at the Met, this time in the role of Amneris, a key character in the opera *Aida*. She is also the first American to perform a role in *Caballeria Rusticana* at the world renowned La Scala Opera House in Milan, Italy.

The schedule of an international opera singer is grueling. As a woman, Marianne has made choices that men in her profession would not have had to make. She has never married, and never had a child. Although her seven nieces and nephews consider her to be the best aunt in the world, she lives her life alone. She has friends all over the globe, and is away from them most of the time. Marianne's goal is to sing until she is about 60 years old. At that time, she would like to become an artistic director for an opera company.

Pat taught Marianne, "It's your gift, but don't ever forget who you are. One day, it will all come to an end, and you will still have to be Marianne Cornetti." And at that point, Marianne, as experienced and accomplished as she is, will have to figure out a way to get into another game.

It's that way for all of us. Careers, like games, are always changing, and we have to repeatedly learn how to get into the game.

There is no formula for success; we must all choose our own paths. We have to learn the rules of the game and how to play them. Every single woman is as important as you are, and she has a story to tell, just like you do. Let's cross some lines together and see what we can experience as women who support and encourage each other.

Rewrite the Rules

Let's write the rules our way in a genuine yet unconventional light:

- **The Rules, They are Always There** – The rules are different. The game is easier to play once you understand the rules.

- **Reframe Your Worth** – Live your dreams. To be without dreams is to be without hope; to be without hope is to be without purpose.

- **Let Your Heart be Your GPS** – Set your own goals based on what is important to you, not what others think is important. Only you know what is best for you.

- **A Little Courage Goes a Long Way** – Embrace risk, and don't be afraid. We learn how to be brave by taking chances.

- **Refuse to Listen to the Chatter** – Don't listen to the negative or limiting words that others speak to you.

- **Change the Script** – Avoid comparing yourself with others. Each of us is different, and each of us is exceptional.

- **God Colored outside the Lines, So Can You** – Be relentless when you have something to offer; never give up. Nothing is really over until the moment you stop trying.

- **The World Needs You** – Live your life from a spirit of abundance. You will become successful by making the people around you successful.

- **Be Lovingly Persistent** – Live your life one day at a time, in the present, each day to its fullest. Don't let your life slip through your fingers by living in the past or for the future.

We should be realistic and, at the same time, understand that we are beautiful and wonderfully complex creations. If we believe in ourselves, and each other, we can each create a life of empowerment, joy, and fulfillment.

And why not put some lipstick on and flash a confident "I'm beautiful inside and out" smile at someone?!

Lipstick Lessons

Appearance is crucial to your success in the workplace, and you must be smart in your dress and presentation.

Your worth is not based on your physical beauty. You are special because of who you are.

There is no formula for success. You must choose your own path.

Lead your own Bragfest. You have unique personal qualities that have helped you achieve great things in the past and those qualities will help you become the woman you want to be.

You got Sizzle baby!

Your Face Isn't Finished Until Your Lipstick is On

Chapter 2

The Rules, They Are Always There

"If you don't like something, change it. If you can't change it, change your attitude." – Maya Angelou

As little girls we were brought up to believe that all we had to do was sit still, smile pretty, be cute, and act smart (although not too smart) and our Prince Charming would arrive at our doorstep.

Really, how many of us didn't think that Cinderella was absolutely the best story ever?

A beautiful little girl who is unloved, forced to work hard all day taking care of her two ugly step-sisters and evil step-mother. Yet even in her terrible hardship she would still believe and sing:

> *A dream is a wish your heart makes*
> *When you're fast asleep*
> *In dreams you will lose your heartaches*
> *Whatever you wish for you keep*

> *Have faith in your dreams and someday*
> *Your rainbow will come smiling through*
> *No matter how your heart is grieving*
> *If you keep on believing*
> *The dream that you wish will come true*

One day a Fairy Godmother magically appeared and, with a flick of her wand, produced the most beautiful gown ever seen, turned a pumpkin into a coach and mice into white horses, so that Cinderella could attend the Royal Ball.

At the ball, the Prince fell madly in love with her. But Cinderella had to flee at midnight before everything turned back to rags, mice, and a pumpkin. In her haste she lost her glass slipper.

The Prince searched the Kingdom high and low to find the girl whose delicate foot would fit into the tiny glass slipper. He found her humble house, and Cinderella married her Prince and lived happily ever after—an undeniable success story.

Prince Charming is Not Coming

In real life, however, success and happiness isn't about wishing and praying that someday a prince will come along and make all your dreams come true. The romantic image of a prince finding his princess, much less fall in love with her, on account of magic shoes sets us up for some unrealistic expectations, especially when we expect to be that princess.

We should remember that these are fictitious characters and avoid romanticizing that our life will turn out happily ever after. Rather, it is up to us to decide what we want. The magic lies in knowing that there is not a "one shoe fits all" formula, but rather that we all can create our own enchanting formula for success.

From childhood, boys and girls play with a different set of rules. Little girls should be nice, and little boys should be strong. Little girls should first attend to the needs of others, and little boys should ask for what they want. And, because men created the rules, we can choose to be successful by playing by their rules—or perhaps it's time to begin creating a new set of rules on our own.

Saboteurs are Among Us

Women face unique challenges in their lives and careers. There really are different rules and expectations reserved just for women:
- Be smart, but not too smart
- Be assertive, but don't ask for too much
- Carry yourself with authority, but don't go too far or risk being labeled the "B" word

Unfortunately, the rules aren't put there entirely by men. I encounter women everyday who snipe, undermine, and sabotage other women's success—usually because they themselves are in a place of insecurity and fear.

In my seminars, I work very hard to make sure the participants get real value from the training. I work to give tips, tools, and techniques that they can use immediately in their work and personal life. Because the seminar companies offer a 100% satisfaction or your money back guarantee, as the seminar leader, I attempt to ensure that every customer leaves the seminar with the information they are seeking. Hours of study and preparation go into each seminar topic.

Early in my speaking career, I received a call from the Faculty Coordinator at one of the seminar companies. She was concerned because two of the women in my class called, requesting their money back.

I clearly remembered the day, and knew there were a couple women who were in and out of the room, late returning from breaks and lunch, and whispering to each other all day. So I wasn't really surprised by her message. I knew in my heart that their money back request wasn't about me. Instead, I believed that they knew the system and they were successfully working it. However, I was shocked by the reason they gave for their dissatisfaction, "The seminar leader put lipstick on in the front of the room."

I laughed out loud when I heard their reason.

Unfortunately, the seminar company representative did not see the humor in the situation. She sternly asked me, "Monica, did you put lipstick on in the front of the room?"

I explained that I always keep a tube of gloss at my front table and will periodically reapply, but only during a break, or when the participants are working on an individual or group assignment and their attention is not on me. She warned me that additional money back requests could cost me speaking contracts and, in the future, to avoid putting lipstick on in front of the participants.

Can we get real here??!! Did it really offend you that that I put on lipstick? And, were you that offended that you couldn't learn anything the entire day and had to request your money back? How can we ever change the rules if we as women insist on placing idealistic or subjective rules on each other?

Until we truly learn to support each other, and focus on the factors that will bring us real success, we will continue to face the rules placed on us by men. And the men's rules are everywhere!

Watch Out for the Bull

My husband, Mark, and I recently attended the Ft. Worth Stock Show and Rodeo. It was such an interesting mix of sights, sounds and smells. Cute cowboys, pretty cowgirls, boots, belt buckles, corn dogs, and patriotism were in abundance.

One of the most interesting events was called the Calf Scramble. Sixteen boys and girls between the age of 14 and 17 entered the arena, each with a rope halter. Eight calves were then released into the arena and each of the participants tried to catch a calf, halter it and lead it across the finish line. Each contestant who got their calf across the finish line won $500!

The calves looked like they weighed 130-150 pounds and they were running and kicking up their heels trying to avoid the scrambling teens. The girls were running around, pony tails bobbing, while the boys tackled the calves and took them down to the ground.

As we watched the spectacle, I commented to Mark, "Why don't the girls work together? They could split the winnings, each earning $250. That's better than the nothing they're getting at this point."

It was painful to watch. The contest ended when some of the arena officials assisted the girls, helping them get their calves across the finish line.

The next morning I checked the newspaper and found that the reason the girls didn't work together was because it was against the rules—another example that we as women live according to the rules established by men. The Calf Scramble Rules read that if a participant catches a calf, no other participant will be allowed to touch the calf unless it breaks free. Furthermore, if two or more participants simultaneously catch the same calf, the calf will be released.

The only way that any of the girls won was because a man stepped in to help them. I'm left wondering what those young women learned:

1. The rules are made by men.

2. You, as a woman, can't bring your initiative or problem-solving skills into the conflict or you'll break the rules.

3. Men, because they made the rules, can break them when you prove yourself inadequate to complete the task as they established it.

4. Men will step in to rescue you. (Rather like Prince Charming, don't you think?)

The contest was challenging. It was supposed to be. However, the deck was definitely stacked against the girls. I question what would have happened if they were allowed to use their natural gifts of cooperation and teamwork. Would they have been able to turn the conflict into collaboration?

Underwear First

It seems that by nature, women tend to know the rules and follow them more so than men.

My friend, Sharon, told me a story about her grandchildren that is a classic example of the difference between girls and boys, and the way we look at rules. Sharon took her two young grandchildren to their swimming lessons, and afterwards, was helping them dry off and get dressed in the locker room.

Her six year old granddaughter, Annalyse, was very aware of the rules and wanted to make sure that her younger brother, Grayson, was following those rules. Plus, she got very annoyed with him when he does not.

Grayson sat down on his towel and started to get dressed by putting his socks on first. This greatly upset Annalyse who said to him, "Grayson that is inappropriate, you are supposed to put your underwear on first."

She turned to Sharon for reinforcement and asked, "Isn't that right, Grandma? It's inappropriate to put your socks on before your underwear. Please tell Grayson he should put his underwear on first."

Sharon encouraged her to just get dressed and leave her brother alone, but Annalyse was insistent that it was "inappropriate."

In response to her statements, Grayson stood up, still with no underwear on, and proceeded to put on his boots. Sharon confided in me that it was all she could do to keep a straight face.

Annalyse was beside herself. After all, she knows the rules and understands how important it is that others follow those rules.

Life definitely has its rules, boundaries, winners, and losers. Men tend to gravitate towards getting the job done. As women, we gravitate toward the rules and to doing it the right way. We tend to play safe rather than play smart.

However, as women, we also bring a unique set of behaviors to life situations. We are great conceptual thinkers; we can see the big picture as well as think between the lines.

The rules are always there, and our tendencies to collaborate rather than compete, listen more than talk, and use relationships rather than muscle to influence, are the very behaviors that will ultimately enable us to change the rules!

Maybe it is time for us to make our own rules, to follow those rules, and, at times, bend them to achieve our own success!

Lipstick Lessons

Prince Charming is not coming, and if he does you'll have to share his attention with the horse.

We need to support, rather than sabotage, each other.

You have natural gifts of collaboration and teamwork; look for opportunities to use them.

It's OK if you don't put your underwear on first.

Chapter 3

Reframe Your Worth

"Always act like you're wearing an invisible crown."
    - Author Unknown

Our black lab very rarely comes in the car with us. Her trips are either to get a vanilla ice cream cone from the nearby Sonic or to visit our oldest son Lou.

One day, as we were backing out of the driveway, I saw Bear staring forlornly at us through the window. It occurred to me that she thought we were either travelling to get ice cream or going to see Lou, and we were leaving her behind.

As far as Bear knows, there are only two reasons to get into a car: to get ice cream or visit Lou. It's all she knows—it's her frame of reference. No wonder she looked so sad watching us pull out of the driveway.

Now sometimes just to tease Bear, I'll wave at her and say, "Bye Bear. See you later. We're going to get ice cream."

We only know what we know. If we think that car trips only end up at Sonic or Lou's house, we can't fathom other possibilities, such as trips to the store, church, or the doctor's. That's the problem with frames of reference; if we get stuck in one, we miss opportunities and new ways of looking at things.

Nothing is as deceptively simple as a frame of reference. On the surface, it seems obvious that in order to make observations, we must do so from a certain point in space and time. Yet, when the implications of this concept are explored, it becomes much more complex.

Your frame of reference about a given topic is what you automatically bring to every conversation and situation you enter. As a result, you usually don't have the option of making your response a conscious choice. It just happens. The challenge is that your frame is limited because it has been built on your experiences and perceptions of reality.

Coming face-to-face with your frame of reference about a situation involves the awareness of your perceptions and an understanding of how these perceptions determine your behavior or actions.

Often, your frame doesn't leave room for new behavior because it's cluttered with perceptions inherited from family, society, friends, and other outside influences.

As a teenager, I remember going to a friend's house for dinner and watching in amazement as her mother served everyone and never sat down at the table for dinner. She had spent hours cooking the meal, and only sat down to eat the leftovers after everyone else had excused themselves from the table.

If you were taught that women should take care of others before they take care of themselves, then you might carry a lot of guilt and stress when trying to spend time on yourself.

When people tell you what you can and cannot do, they are speaking from their frame of reference. That's their perception. It doesn't have to be yours.

For example, I have a friend who, when growing up, was told she needed to be protected from the big bad things of the world; consequently, she was not often allowed to experience things first hand without a "big brother" type of friend with her. She jokingly adds that she doesn't remember her real brother having to take a "big sister" friend along with him on his adventures.

Today, many women support themselves and their family. However, if you've been taught you can't do it unless you have a man by your side, how much more difficult is it to believe and have confidence in your own abilities?

Expand Your Frame

Creating a new frame of reference allows you to consider new possibilities. It will ignite creativity, energy, and enthusiasm. It will inspire you to stretch your thinking to create something new.

The key to expanding your frame of reference is choosing to do so.

Who makes the decisions in your life? Do you create your own success? Are you loving what you're doing and doing what you love?

Your frame of reference is always based on where you are at a particular point in space and time. It usually depends on where you're sitting.

On a flight to California recently, the pilot came on and made an announcement saying, "For those passengers sitting on the right hand side of the plane, if you look out your window, you'll see a great view of the Grand Canyon. And for those passengers sitting on the left hand side of the plane, (pause) if you'll look to your right, you'll see those passengers looking out their window at a great view of the Grand Canyon."

The reality is, if you don't like the view from your frame of reference, it may be time to change your seat.

Perform Before Kings

There is a scripture that says, "Do you see a man skilled in his work. He will stand before kings; he will not stand before obscure men." Actually, that scripture has always bothered me; I would have preferred to be the king, rather than performing my skill in front of him.

When I started my speaking career, my first paying gig was a contract to teach Management Skills for Non-Managers. I was very excited about the opportunity to get out there and change people's lives. After all, I had years of experience managing and leading people, and knew that I had a lot of information that would help my participants improve their management skills.

It was a mid-February day when I boarded a plane to Indiana. By the time I landed, it was dark and I still had a two hour drive to my destination city, Kokomo. When I arrived at the hotel, it was not quite what I had expected—a little run down, but I thought, well let's just see how this goes. The man at the front desk checked me in and told me to drive my car around to the back of the hotel, as it would provide better access to my room.

I tried to maintain a positive attitude. I went in search of my room, dragging my luggage down a dark staircase at the back of the hotel, proceeding down a narrow hallway, still looking for my room.

And there it was. Once I pushed through the door, and fumbled for the light switch, I found a room that failed to meet my expectations. The carpet was raggedy, the wallpaper was peeling from the walls, and the bedspread was frayed. I sat down on the edge of an ottoman wishing I had brought some Lysol disinfectant spray.

Glancing to my right, I saw that my window was ground level with the parking lot. Even with the curtains pulled completely closed, there was still a good inch gap around the edges and anyone walking by could easily see into my room.

As I perched on the ottoman, one thought ran on an endless loop in my mind, "What was I thinking? Why did I think that public speaking and seminar training was a good idea?" Remembering that I had a roll of packing tape in my bag, I rifled for it and proceeded to tape the curtain to the wall, so as to block outside viewers. Then I sat once again on the ottoman and repeated to myself, "What was I thinking?"

Isn't most of life like that? We have a picture in our mind of how an experience or event is going to look like, but reality usually ends up much different. It is like the excitement we felt as children waiting for Christmas day to arrive; we could hardly get to sleep on Christmas Eve.

I remember my sister and I playing an endless game of "race you to the bottom of the bed" because we were simply too excited to close our eyes.

That's the same kind of excitement I had felt as I prepared to go out on that first seminar. I looked forward to the crowds of adoring fans as I traveled from lovely location to beautiful hotel.

But the reality was a rundown hotel in Kokomo, Indiana.

The next morning I got up and prepared for the day of training. I looked forward to meeting my first room of participants, and was ready to teach them everything I knew about management skills in six hours.

Then I faced another rude awakening; although the women attending the seminar were nice and friendly, I found that for the most part they had been sent by their boss to learn skills they weren't really interested in learning. They were quite happy to stay the way they were.

I was puzzled. How could this be? How can you NOT want to gain new skills and knowledge as you climb the ladder to success? I remember thinking— I don't know who these people are. I cannot relate to them.

I had to change my frame of reference. As a novice speaker, I wanted to teach them what they didn't want to learn. I couldn't change them, but I could change my point of view.

As I have worked hard to improve my skills as a speaker and seminar leader, I have found that there is a direct correlation between my skills and the type of people that I speak to. As my skills increase, I may not be performing before kings, but I now have the opportunity to speak to entrepreneurs, leaders, and CEO's of large companies.

By changing my point of view, I found new opportunities. And while I still have participants who resist change, I have had many chances to help those who are looking for new tools, knowledge, and skills.

Change Your Vantage Point

You may have been born or placed into a certain position in life—and if you are not happy with that seat, it might be time to change your vantage point.

Who makes your decisions for you? As women, we naturally seek security, and have paid the price for that by giving away our freedom. You may have gotten married because you wanted to achieve a certain lifestyle and didn't think you could do that on your own. You may have chosen the security of a job, and now someone is telling you what to do. You may have security, but your employer decides what time you can go home to be with your family, when you can take a vacation, eat lunch, and even when you can drink a cup of coffee.

Life becomes a habit of waiting for others to give us permission. We hesitate to ask for what we need or want. If your frame is too small, it will limit the scope of your dreams and your achievements. It will squelch your creativity, energy, enthusiasm, and passion. If the frame is wider, it can inspire you to stretch your thinking to create something new.

Creating a new frame of reference is challenging and requires a willingness to create a new mindset and consider new possibilities. We have to discard old frameworks and elevate our thinking to create new ones.

Recently, my son Nick was held up at gun point. He was scared, but the overwhelming emotion he felt was one of confusion. Nick has always been the person who believes the best of others and is always for the underdog. He sees himself as 'one with the universe.'

As the young boy, not older than 16, held the gun to Nick's chest, Nick looked at him and said, "Dude! We're brothers – why are you doing this?"

The thief, of course, didn't want to hear such talk. When the driver of the getaway vehicle yelled "Just cap him", Nick realized that his life was in real danger. Fortunately, he was not harmed, but they did get away with his credit cards, cash, and iPhone.

Later when we talked about the incident, I realized that Nick was most disappointed by the fact that he now had to create a new frame of reference. He had to realize that not everyone was his brother, and there are people out there who will steal from him.

Interestingly, Nick's heart chooses to still see the best in people, and believe that, at their core, people are good. However, I now see a higher level of maturity in him when dealing with others. I am proud of his positive response to a terrible situation.

Broaden Your Beliefs

The key to changing your frame of reference is choosing to do so. Uncovering any of your limiting beliefs, while challenging the expectations put on you by others, will not be an easy task. Commit to improving your skills, trying new things, and surrounding yourself with people who are encouraging you to change.

I see women in my seminar rooms who have spent a lifetime taking care of everyone else. The past 20 years of their life have been spent juggling kids, supporting their husbands' career, and cleaning up after everyone. They've prepared dinners, packed lunches, kissed hurts, and an endless list of other things—most times in addition to holding a down a full-time job.

Now the kids have grown up and moved away. The house is quiet, and stays cleaner longer. Their husbands are busy, and the women wonder, "What's next?" They feel empty – like their life's purpose has ended with another 40 to 50 years left to live. This can be devastating, and many women resolve that "this is it and this is all there is ever going to be."

The reality is that now is the time to change your frame of reference, to push ahead for new horizons, get a second wind, and go for it. The opportunity is now in front of you to find a passion area that will give your life a new meaning.

If I just described you, understand that a new frame of reference isn't going to be drawn easily. There is no cookie-cutter, step-by-step process to arrive at a life of meaning.

Start by finding something that you particularly enjoy and begin developing your skill and expertise in that area. As you perfect your skill or talent, others will begin to notice how good you are at it. The more others notice your ability, the more you love it, and before you know it, your passion is born.

Obstacles, They are Everywhere

A word of caution: on your journey to finding your passion and purpose, you will encounter obstacles that may cause you to think that you cannot create a new frame. These obstacles may come in the form of family and friends who don't support your undertaking, a lack of knowledge, money, or time, and many other challenges that could get in your way.

When faced with these challenges, remind yourself to be patient. It took time for you to get to this point, and you aren't going to create a new frame overnight.

One of the most important ways I've found to stay on course is to listen to my heart. If you start down a path and your spirit seems uneasy, or something about the direction doesn't feel right to you, stop, and make the necessary adjustments to get back on track.

Finding and pursuing your passion will bring a new joy and meaning to your life. You'll feel like you are contributing and really making a difference in the world.

I challenge you to take the risk, dream big dreams, and create a frame of reference as a woman who leaves a legacy of passion and fulfillment.

Begin today to reframe your worth and choose to see yourself from a new point of view.

Lipstick Lessons

You only know what you know, and you evaluate all of life through that frame.

Reframe your reality if you don't like the view from your frame of reference.

You can ask for what you want. You don't have to wait for others to give you permission.

Commit to improving your skills and surround yourself with others who encourage you to grow.

Find your passion, follow your heart, and reframe your worth.

Your Face Isn't Finished Until Your Lipstick is On

Chapter 4

Let Your Heart be Your GPS

"We are not what we know but what we are willing to learn."
 - Mary Catherine Bateson

What if you could spend your life doing exactly what you love to do, and make money doing it?

Many people work in jobs they hate; they feel trapped. So why don't they just quit and pursue what they love to do? Two reasons: they don't know what they want to do, and they have an intense fear of failure.

For me, the first issue, not knowing what I wanted to do, plagued me. I always wanted to be a professional business woman; at the same time, I had the picture in my mind that I would be the "Kool-aid Mom," you know, the cool mom on the block who is always smiling and serving the kids cookies, offering fun activities, and helping them solve their problems.

The two goals simply didn't line up, so I thought I would just put the professional business woman dream on the shelf for a couple years.

The challenge was that in the middle of what should have been my Kool-aid Mom period, I let other people decide what I should do.

I was asked to take the position of Business Administrator at a large non-profit organization. The reality was that it was more than just mere asking; influential people in my life regularly pressured me to take the position. Finally, one afternoon, I decided that I should accept the job. I naively stepped into a role that was much bigger than I could have ever imagined.

No matter how many hours I worked, there was always something else that needed to be done. Unfortunately, I became an enabler of the system; regardless of what it took, I was always sure to complete the projects on time.

I made choices that kept me away from home for long hours. Even when I was home, my thoughts were distracted from my family.

At the end of that period, I thought that I had "wasted" 10 years of my life. But of course, those years weren't a waste. I met and worked with some of my favorite people in the world. The people who worked side-by-side with me in my department and on special projects earned a permanent spot in my heart. Even though we seldom see or talk to each other today, if any of them called me at 3:00 a.m. and needed something, I would drop everything to help them.

During the 10-years working in a career that I never wanted, I learned about business, leadership, and negotiations. I was able to achieve great things that others before me had not been able to do. And I use that experience today in my seminars.

But at the time, I never sat down to determine what it was I really wanted to do.

I know now that I was not so different from other women. Most women can tell you what they don't want; very few can actually articulate what they want.

Unfortunately, life is unpredictable. Unexpected events can dramatically alter the course of your life. A change in trends, a personal tragedy, or an oversight with untimely consequences—any of these can change your life's path.

In the face of these challenges, you must decide the direction to steer your life in. Otherwise, you leave yourself wide open for others to direct and dictate your life. Their plan will never be as good as the map you would have drawn for yourself. When the detours come, and they will, it will be easier to get back on course if you have a clear vision of where you are headed.

What are You Afraid Of?

Once you determine what it really is you want to do, it's time to identify the fears that are holding you back.

Although fear can get in the way of you achieving your hopes, dreams, and desires, fear is not always a bad thing. It does have a real purpose. It helps keep us safe and keeps us from taking dangerous risks.

For many though, fear runs their lives. Whether it is fear of failure, rejection, public speaking, flying, escalators, or any other phobia, it keeps us from living our lives to the fullest.

There are basically three categories of fear: real, imagined, and worry. "Real" fear often acts as the universe's warning signal. It is a concern that is based in reality and causes you to evaluate the potential risks for some very good reasons.

For instance, feeling "afraid" to start your own business when you do not have sufficient financial reserves is a healthy fear. It is a word of warning to get your finances in order before pursuing your new venture.

The second category, "imagined" fear, is not healthy. This type of fear is in our head. When we hear those fears we have to consider whether they are truly reasonable, or are they an excuse for not trying something new. Imagined fear keeps us from doing what needs to be done to achieve our goals.

Do any of these statements sound familiar to you?

"I'm too old."
"It will take too long."
"I won't be any good at it."
"That's not a career for women."
"People will laugh."

Most imagined fears are based on either the fear of failure or the fear of rejection. If you spend all your time fearing failure or rejection, you can never move forward.

The third category of fear is plain old "worry." It's the most pervasive form of fear, and it saps your time and energy. There is plenty to worry about—swine flu, the unemployment rate, credit card debt, health insurance, or choosing the right school for your child.

Worry is pointless and counterproductive. It leeches time and energy away from achieving your goals. Imagine how much more you could achieve if worry wasn't nagging in your mind. Instead of spending energy on worrying, use it to take action.

Get Ready to Jump!

Admitting you are afraid of something is the first step toward analyzing whether it is a real or imagined fear, or just plain worry. You have the opportunity to evaluate what is really holding you back.

My youngest son, Joe, has worked hard his entire life to keep up with his two older brothers. One summer vacation, when the boys were pre-teens, we rented a lovely condo that sat directly on the banks of the Comal River in New Braunfels, TX. The Comal is a spring fed river, so it is ice cold and crystal clear; wonderful for tubing, swimming, and snorkeling.

At the river entry point, there is a 10-foot stone wall that kids use as a launch pad to jump into the river. My two oldest boys were quick to take the plunge and were having a blast jumping into the icy water. They would yell encouragements to Joe to jump off the wall into the river below.

"Encourage" is probably too mild a word. They coaxed, cajoled, and teased, but nothing worked. Joe would walk to the edge, ready to take the plunge, but would lose his courage at the last minute and back away. This went on for what seemed like forever. He would walk to the edge once again, start to jump, but then turn at the last minute and move back to safety.

Aren't we the same way when trying to find the courage we need to take the risk and make a big change in our lives? We want to change, but it would mean taking a leap into unknown waters. We keep getting close to the edge, but few of us ever muster the courage to take the plunge.

By the way, Joe did finally jump off the rock wall and spent a great day jumping and swimming in the river. In his 20's now, Joe was first in line to jump off the 100-foot high rock cliff at Waimea Bay during our recent trip to Hawaii.

Overcoming fear is one of the most important things you can do to lay the groundwork for success in those areas of your life where you want to make a change. When you are fearful, your focus is on what could go wrong, rather than picturing success and the rewards that will come with it.

Just for Today . . .

Recently, I was speaking to a management team and some of our discussion centered on dealing with the negative emotions of worry and fear. We talked about how worry and fear can immobilize us. When we worry, we lose the power to focus on solutions; instead, we focus on the problem to the point that all we can see is the problem.

I worry about achieving my goals. I've been doing a lot of goal setting lately as I map out a plan for financial security. It seems like such an easy thing to do until I have to break it down into monthly revenue goals. That's where it falls apart for me.

I begin to worry if I'm positioning myself in the right place, with the right people, to achieve my goals. The calculations on whether or not I'll be able to drive enough revenue for my business next year creates a desire to pull the covers over my head and recite my favorite Scarlett O'Hara line, "I'll worry about that tomorrow." And worry I will.

As I continue this process of growing my independent speaking and training business, I can find plenty of opportunity to worry about goals and potential failure. My ability to achieve "financial success" rides on my ability to book enough gigs in my calendar, at a speaking fee sufficient enough that I don't have to be on the road every day of the year.

I've always set high goals, and if I don't reach those goals, I often think of myself as a failure. I was taught by a mentor that excuses and excellence don't mix … so I am not one who is willing to settle for an excuse when I don't achieve a goal. But that doesn't mean I don't give myself plenty of opportunity to worry along the way.

So how do you stop worrying? The key to overcoming worry is to learn new patterns. When you find yourself beginning to worry, stop and pay attention to the physical symptoms and thoughts that accompany that process. Now, switch your thinking to the present and focus on what you can do right now.

I did an activity with a management team that I have been working on applying in my own life. I had them write down this phrase and repeat it aloud several times to the people at their table, "Just for today, I will not worry." You could see everyone breathe easier as they recited the line. If we, like Scarlett O'Hara, can postpone our worrying until tomorrow, it will give our brains an entire day's rest from worry and a chance to focus on solutions.

Hairy Monsters

Get to know your fears.

Most people are aware of their fears, but they never really identify where they come from and why they have them. For example, if you have a fear of failure, what gave birth to that fear? There is a cause for everything, so spend some time and track down the origins of your fear.

Knowing where your fear comes from is the biggest key to understanding it. Understanding your fears is good because it also means that you will be able to work on finding solutions to conquer those fears.

Talk to a friend about your fear. Often times the simple act of vocalizing it causes the fear to start to disappear. Inside, the fear is a huge, hairy monster that we are afraid to face. Once we start talking about it, and putting it into perspective, we can then develop strategies to deal with it. Speaking aloud will make you feel stronger and more prepared to face your fear and control it. That huge, hairy monster may actually be a tiny fur ball that is easily swept away.

Identifying your fears, and understanding why they exist, will enable you to take the next step: facing your fears!

When you feel strong enough to face those fears, go for it. It will be difficult, and perhaps you won't succeed in your first couple of attempts, but, with practice and persistence, you will eventually reduce that fear to a mere memory and have the strength to face other challenges.

The first time I spoke in front of a group of people, I was so nervous that I was sure I would pass out. With palms sweating and knees shaking, I felt my heart pounding so hard, I was sure you could see my suit jacket move with every beat.

Now, I look for opportunities to speak, and the bigger the audience the better! Sure, I still get nervous because I want my message to be relevant to the lives of the participants. I figure if I ever stop getting the pre-platform jitters, then it's time for me to find another profession. Besides, within the first few minutes, the jitters are gone and we're all having fun together.

Facing your fears may take time, but it will be worth it when you see how dramatically your life changes. You will be able to face the world more open-mindedly. You will begin doing the things you have always wanted to do.

But when you allow fear to control your life, you miss out on a world of new and valuable opportunities. The truth is, you may never eliminate your fears entirely, but you will learn to take charge and decide just how much you will allow fear to be a part of your life.

Decide today what it is you really want. Identify and face your fears. Decide to take charge of your destiny. Let your heart guide you.

I am convinced that taking charge of your destiny by making your own choices requires more courage than most of us are willing to muster. As we go through life, it is much easier and more comfortable to conform to what we've been told is the right thing to do, rather than stand up and choose what is best for us.

So, commit to following the desires of your heart. Put them to good use, use them to bless someone else, begin achieving your goals, and start enjoying your life.

Lipstick Lessons

Life is unpredictable; decide what direction you want to steer your life.

You can never move forward if you spend all your time fearing failure or rejection.

Just for today, **do not worry**.

Identify and face your fears. They probably are not as scary as you think.

Follow the desires of your heart; you may be surprised where they take you!

Chapter 5

A Little Courage Goes a Long Way

"The best way to gain self-confidence is to do what you are afraid to do." - Author Unknown

Life is full of obstacles – some are there because of choices we've made, and some pop up courtesy of circumstances beyond our control. In either case, when we encounter the obstacles, we have to decide whether to fall apart, or figure out a way to overcome the obstacles. Will we choose to be a victim of our circumstances, or to succeed in the midst of life's painful lessons?

We all know that bad things happen to good people—the death of a child or a spouse, a painful divorce, a diagnosis of cancer. The bottom line is everyone, at some point in their life, will run straight into a wall they haven't encountered before; the kind of wall that knocks you down and leaves you feeling like you will never be able to get up again. The best we can do is roll over in pain and draw up the courage to pick ourselves up and move on; because, if not, we'll get stuck in a victim mentality and act as if we're trapped, with no options and no way out.

Courage is an interesting concept to me. Many times I don't have the courage to speak up when I should. I often don't have the courage to follow through on an idea, a plan, or even a phone call to a perspective client.

There is one incident that particularly stands out in my memory, because it was a classic example of my lack of courage. I was in an Executive Board Meeting with a room full of men. We were discussing major projects and upcoming deadlines. During our discussion, it was discovered that we were going to miss a major deadline that would dramatically jeopardize the success of numerous projects surrounding this event. At that point, my boss lost his temper and accused me, quite vehemently, of dropping the ball.

While my boss ranted, raved, and yelled at me, the man who was actually responsible for missing the deadline sat right next to me and never spoke up.

At the time, I did not have the courage to say anything; instead, I did what all professional business women dread. I broke into tears. My tears turned into full blown sobs, complete with hyperventilating. I didn't have the courage to get up and walk out of the room. Of course, the rest of the people in the room were extremely uncomfortable.

As women, we need to avoid substituting tears for appropriately responding to anger. Women often cry because we've been taught that expressing anger is not ladylike or acceptable. And in those tears, we accept others' anger and diminish our position.

In that board meeting, I was angry—angry that my boss was yelling at me in front of a room full of my colleagues; angry that his accusation was not accurate; and angry that the true culprit was a bigger weenie than me. The man may have not broken into tears, but the reality was he didn't have an ounce more courage than I; he just didn't proceed to make a fool of himself over it.

When I first started to cry, I should have immediately excused myself, instead of staying and bawling out of control. By removing myself from the situation, I could have allowed myself the chance to compose my thoughts.

That was a turning point in my career. I vowed that I would never allow anything like that to happen to me again. I started reading books and taking classes on assertive communication and negotiation skills at a local women's group. The class helped me muster the courage to speak up when faced with a similar situation.

I learned that it would have been better for everyone if I had been able to calmly reply to my boss, saying something like, "I'm confused as to why you are yelling at me. It was my understanding that I was responsible for this list of items. I've given you the status report on each of them. If you want me to be responsible for Project Y, let's look at adding that to my list."

I wouldn't have had to point a finger or assign blame to the person who was really responsible for the assignment. If I had used an approach like this, I may have gained the respect of my boss and we might have developed a plan for moving forward.

A Negotiating Fool!

The more I learned in my class on assertive communication, the more my courage grew. I learned things like never asking for something before you know what you want, making sure you are talking to the decision maker, and always giving them a choice. After the class, I felt better prepared to handle my next challenge.

A few weeks following the class, I was scheduled to speak in Wisconsin. Because of the flight schedules, I determined that it would take me more time to fly the second leg of my flight than it would to simply rent a car and drive to my destination. So I gathered my bags, left the airport, rented a car, and drove to my destination.

Unbeknownst to me, by not taking the second leg of the flight, I automatically cancelled out my return flight home.

I showed up at the airport Friday evening, eager to get home after a long week on the road. As I attempted to check in, the system would not allow me to. It said that I had to see an agent. I patiently waited in line for an agent, and when it was finally my turn, the agent explained that I had cancelled my flight.

I took a deep breath and thought to myself, "You can handle this." I pulled out the classic negotiating question opener I had learned at my class, and asked the agent, "What would have to be true for me to be able to get on my flight home?"

She looked at me and said, "You'll have to pay $695."

Now my heart stopped, as I thought to myself, "Not good!"

Determined to apply my newly acquired negotiating skills, I remembered that I needed to be speaking to the decision maker. The agent was just doing her job and following the rules.

I asked her if I could speak with her manager, and she informed that they were in the middle of a shift change and it would be 15-20 minutes. Since I wasn't going anywhere anyhow, I smiled and said I'd be happy to wait.

Besides, that gave me time to prepare my negotiating strategy, work up my courage, and practice what I was going to say. I felt surprisingly calm. I believed I was going to be able to achieve my objective of getting on that flight home. At the same time, there was an underlying nervousness because I was thinking, "$695 is a lot of money! That will really hurt if I have to pay that."

Finally, the agent motioned to me that the manager was on his way. I took a deep breath, put a smile on my face, and walked to meet him. I shook his hand and he asked me, "How can I help you?"

Unbelievably, my response was an instant fountain of tears! I started crying, explaining, "I cancelled my flight home when I rented a car. She said it's going to cost me $695. I didn't mean to do that." On and on — an endless stream of tears, and not a single negotiating strategy in sight.

He let out a deep sigh and said, "Follow me." He went behind the counter, printed out my ticket, and handed it to me.

I continued to cry as I thanked him over and over. He just patted me on the shoulder, and walked away.

I was so disappointed in my response. I didn't even come close to using the techniques I learned. Instead, I was right back where I started.

Why are You Crying?

A little boy asked his mother, "Why are you crying?"

She paused to reassure her son. "Because I'm a woman," she told him.

"I don't understand," he said.

His Mom just hugged him and said, "And you never will."

Later the little boy asked his father, "Why does mother seem to cry for no reason?"

"All women cry for no reason," was all his dad could say.

The little boy grew up and became a man, still wondering why women cry. He put in a call to God. When God got on the phone, he asked, "God, why do women cry so easily?"

God said, "When I made woman, she had to be special.

"I made her shoulders strong enough to carry the weight of the world, yet gentle enough to give comfort.

"I gave her an inner strength to endure childbirth, and the rejection that many times comes from her children.

"I gave her a hardness that allows her to keep going when everyone else gives up, and take care of her family through sickness and fatigue without complaining.

"I gave her the sensitivity to love her children under any and all circumstances, even when they have hurt her very badly.

"I gave her strength to carry her husband through his faults, and fashioned her from his rib to protect his heart.

"I gave her wisdom to know that a good husband never hurts his wife, but sometimes tests her strengths and her resolve to stand beside him unfalteringly.

"And finally, I gave her tears to shed. This is hers exclusively to use whenever it is needed.

"You see my son," said God, "the beauty of a woman is not in the clothes she wears, the figure that she carries, or the way she combs her hair. The beauty of a woman must be seen in her eyes, because that is the doorway to her heart–the place where love resides."

Women cry when they're happy, frustrated, excited, and angry. And while most of us know that we shouldn't cry at work, there are times when we just can't help it. Unfortunately, it hurts us professionally. Men can cry, women cannot! To rephrase a line from Tom Hanks in *A League of Their Own*, "There's no crying in baseball—or in the workplace." At least not for women. It seems like men can cry and be admired for it.

I remember watching in wonder when Mark Ingram of the University of Alabama was chosen to receive the 2009 Heisman Trophy Award. He was overcome with emotion. As he struggled through his acceptance speech, he was barely able to thank his parents, team, and coaches. Here was a man who reportedly stood 5'10" and weighed 215 pounds, crying "like a little girl." Although there were a few snide blogs the next day, for the most part, people admired him for his display of emotions.

When women cry, men blame hormones and PMS. The bottom line is men are disturbed by women who cry.

I've learned that crying and courage are not necessarily related. Sometimes, we cry just to cry. Courage, on the other hand, is a way of life. It is as much a habit as anything else. The real test of courage is in our daily lives. The courage to stand up for what we believe in, speak our mind, and not stay silent because we are afraid of what people will say.

Courage is Not the Absence of Fear

According to Mark Twain, "Courage is not the absence of fear. It is acting in spite of it." The sign of a courageous person is someone who feels fear and still goes on to do what they believe is right.

I've found that it's helpful to draw on those characteristics and traits that have helped you succeed in the past. When have you had to draw on your courage, tenacity, faith, determination, daring, or confidence? Remember your sizzle. Courage will begin to rise when you realize you are capable and competent to meet any circumstance head on.

If you can remind yourself of times when you have been able to apply your Sizzle to manage a change or to gather courage, you will begin to feel more powerful and have a greater sense of control in your life.

Steps to Find Courage

I believe a lot of people planned to live a life much different from the one they live today. Life has a way of taking twists and turns that can throw us off balance. If you lose your courage, and begin making poor choices, before you know it, you are in a mess.

Over the years, I've learned a few important steps that may help you find the courage to face your failures.

First, give yourself permission to hurt. When you fail, it hurts. It takes time to work through any anger or grief that you associate with that failure.

Second, give yourself time to heal. Don't try to rush it. Rely on your faith, your friends, and your family for support and strength.

Third, accept that failure is a part of life. As you go through the different stages of your life, you can count on one thing—failure. Learn from failure, grow from it, and take a fresh look at it. Even when darkness surrounds you, identify what you are going to do differently in your life as a result of experiencing that failure.

Fourth, look forward. Do not give in to the temptation to dwell on the past. Fix your eyes on what lies ahead. The universe has many wonderful things in store for you. Focus on your future.

Fifth, find your purpose—your "uniquely you." You were created with sizzle. Part of finding your courage is learning what to do when you hit the wall. Courageous women will find a way to go over it, under it, around it, or through it.

Live life with passion because without it, you are simply going through the motions. If you've not yet discovered the passion that drives you to action, it's time to go find out.

The things we desire in life often seem just out of reach. To get there, you have to gather your courage and step out in faith.

I had the opportunity several years ago to take a risk and pursue my dream. By stepping out of my comfort zone, I found a career that exceeded my wildest expectations. I can tell you, with a little courage, you will experience a life more wonderful than you can imagine right now.

Lipstick Lessons

Life is full of obstacles; when you encounter one, you can choose to fall apart or figure out a way to overcome it.

Avoid substituting tears for a more appropriate response to your emotions, such as assertively confronting whatever is frustrating you.

You will cry for no apparent reason. If you are at work and feel the tears coming on, excuse yourself until you are composed.

Use your Sizzle to gather your courage and you will feel more powerful.

A courageous woman is one who **feels fear and still goes on to do what she believes is right.**

Your Face Isn't Finished Until Your Lipstick is On

Chapter 6

Refuse to Listen to the Chatter

"I was told that whistling wasn't ladylike, but I knew even then that women were simply not supposed to be that happy." - Anonymous

Sticks and stones may break my bones, but words will never hurt me. Have you ever stopped to actually think about this phrase?

The power of the spoken word is real, and we seldom stop to think of the power of our words and the influence they have on others. Words paint pictures, create impressions, and set expectations. I was reminded of this on a recent visit with my sister Melanie.

I called her to make plans and said, "Let's do something fun this Saturday." I was careful to clarify what I meant, because my idea of a "fun" Saturday is meeting at a coffee shop and then antique shopping.

Her idea of a fun Saturday is biking 40 miles, followed by a 10 mile run.

My sister is 18 months older than me. We are about as different as two sisters can be, and always have been. From the time we were small kids, I was the "chubby, pretty sister," and Melanie was the "thin, athletic sister."

I keep a picture on my refrigerator that was taken when my sister and I were three and four years old. To others, it is just a cute picture of two sisters playing in the backyard. To me, it represents words spoken to me that shaped my life.

The picture on my refrigerator is in black and white, so you cannot see what I remember. At three years old, already considered too chubby to wear a bikini, I was forced to wear the most hideous, ugly, navy blue tank suit ever made. Not wanting to draw attention to my belly and thighs, I guess my mom thought if she put me in that navy blue suit, it would make me look thinner.

Because Melanie was skinny, she got to wear a very pretty pink and white gingham bikini.

I remember thinking it was the cutest thing I had ever seen. It even had ruffles! I was so sad because her suit was amazingly cute and mine was simply dreadful. Everyone knew I was the "frou-frou" girl. Ruffles didn't matter to Melanie, yet there she was getting to be all sweet and feminine, while I was given the "suit for chubby girls."

Melanie has always been fearless and athletic. She played field hockey and ran track all through high school. Today she is a top-ranked, national duathlete.

As for me, chubby has stayed with me my entire life. I was the prissy sister involved in choir, band, and theater. I never really got involved in sports.

On that Saturday, when Melanie and I met to have my type of "fun." We reminisced about our childhood and I said to her, "You have no idea what it was like growing up as the fat sister."

The look on her face was one of confusion as she said to me, "What are you talking about? All I ever heard growing up was how pretty you are."

We stared at each other. Neither one of us realized the other had heard such labels as children. Instead of hearing how pretty I was, I had been compared to Melanie's physique. Instead of being praised for her athletic accomplishments, Melanie heard how she fell short of the feminine ideal. Each of us had carried the negative comments of our childhood into adulthood.

Words Have Energy

Behind every word flows energy. Have you thought about your ability to persuade and impact the people in your life? Do your words build up or tear down? Do others feel motivated and inspired after speaking with you? As a person of influence, you must choose your words carefully.

Choose your words carefully. Words have the power to heal broken hearts, make dreams come true, and make someone feel better about themselves. The thoughts you're conveying may not seem life altering to you, but it's not what you say, it's what people hear. If they hear positive, encouraging and uplifting talk, their spirit will align with it. Likewise, if they hear negative talk, or put downs, their spirit will align with the negative comment.

My fourth grade teacher was the first person to plant a seed in me about my future and career. She told me that I was going to go to college, become a teacher, and do great things.

Because I loved this teacher, I accepted those words without question, and believed them from that point forward. If anyone asked me in high school what I was going to do after graduation, I would respond with complete confidence and self assurance, "I'm going to be a teacher."

When my parents and I began to search for colleges, I focused on the institutions with a good reputation for their education department. After several visits, I chose Seton Hill College in Greensburg, PA.

At Seton Hill, the education program was designed so that you majored in one subject and then also enrolled in education classes to receive your Certification in Education; in essence, you had a double major. I decided on Psychology with an Early Childhood/Elementary Certification and immersed myself in the course load.

As a sophomore, I had my first practicum, and was assigned a second grade class at the local Catholic School. When I walked into the classroom, it was wall-to-wall kids. I believe there were 32 children in all.

Now, although I had been told and believed I was going to be a teacher since I was in 4th grade, I had no real-world experience. The teacher introduced me to the class and said, "Monica is studying to be a teacher, and she is going to teach your phonics lesson today." And then, she promptly left the room.

I remember thinking, "Where are you going? You can't leave me here with all these kids!"

I stood in front of a sea of expectant faces and panic overtook me as I thought, "Phonics!! What is phonics? How do you even spell it? F-o-n-i-x?"

I then saw a chart hanging on the back wall with a menagerie of pictures titled "Words that end in at." I thought, "Well let's start there."

"OK kids, let's work on this chart together and see how many words we can come up with that end in at."

At, Bat, Cat, Dat, Fat.

One know-it-all kid piped up and said "Dat is NOT a word."

I stopped, thought for a second, and then said, "Yes it is. Haven't you ever said, 'What's up with dat'?"

They looked at me skeptically, but we kept going.

On my way back to Seton Hill that day, I thought, "Well I lived through *dat*. It can only get better from here as I learn more." After all, I was meant to be a teacher. The words that had been spoken to me, and repeated for the past ten years, gave the assurance that I could overcome obstacles.

As it turned out, my career wasn't as mapped out as I thought it was. At the end of my sophomore year, the advisor for the education department called me into her office and told me she thought I should revise my degree plan because teaching was not for me. Her reasoning? "You do not have the charisma that is necessary to be a teacher."

It was as if she had slapped me across the face. I thought, "I don't have charisma? What does that mean?" It turns out, words also have the power to tear down, break hearts, kill enthusiasm, and keep dreams from coming true.

I allowed my advisor's words to change my life for the next 20 years. Those poorly chosen words, by an influential adult in my life, changed what I had believed to be true.

Has this happened to you? You have a dream, a passion, a mission, and, when you share your idea with someone in your life, they manage to crush it by the words that they speak to you.

The words of others have power over your own thoughts and actions. The same is true about the words you speak to others. As a woman, who influences countless people around you, it is important to always choose your words carefully.

The reality is I do have charisma! I am one of the most dynamic and interactive trainers that you will ever encounter. The participants in my seminar room laugh, cry, discuss, and debate. I love teaching! Today I teach adults, but I didn't get back into the field until I was in my 40's because of the words of one influential person.

One of the most profound powers we have, in both our business and personal life, is the power of our words. The way we talk to people shapes our relationships, and these relationships shape our life.

The Abundance of Your Heart

Unfortunately, there is no formula to ensure that our words are encouraging or gracious. The Bible says that from the abundance of our hearts, our mouths speak, so we know that whatever comes out of our mouths is from our heart.

Words are very powerful whether they are said in love or hate, purposefully or accidentally. Our words have the ability to both hurt and heal. We should be careful to guard our hearts and not let those with negative words into our inner circle, where they may have significant influence.

My sister-in-law's early years were full of music. In the sixth grade, Marianne was given the opportunity to sing a solo, and chose "I'd Like to Teach the World to Sing."

Her older brothers said, "Marianne has such a loud voice!" Even with their teasing, she found a teacher and began to formally study music theory and vocal techniques. From that point there was no turning back.

Marianne attended the Manhattan School of Music immediately after high school, and the culture shock was overwhelming. This was a girl who had grown up on a dirt road where everyone left their keys in the car and their homes unlocked 24 hours a day. By contrast, the Manhattan School of Music is in Harlem. There were no dorms at the time, so Marianne rented a room from a bipolar alcoholic who would threaten her and lock her out of the apartment.

Worse, influential people in her life tried to manipulate Marianne with their words. For instance, one day, in conversation with a vocal coach she had known most of her life, Marianne expressed her frustrations and fears about her life in Harlem. The coach told her, "If you leave the Manhattan School of Music, I will never love you again."

Marianne knew in her heart she had to leave the school, no matter what this person threatened. In fact, she left before the end of her first semester and went to the Cincinnati Conservatory.

But life continued to throw struggles at Marianne. At the Cincinnati Conservatory, she came down with a terrible thyroid problem. She had to drop out of school for yet another year.

When Marianne felt healthy enough, she re-registered at the Conservatory. During her drive back to the conservatory, only thirty miles outside of Cincinnati, she lost her nerve, turned around, and drove all the way home.

Her parents asked her what she was going to do and Marianne replied, "I don't think I want to be a singer any more."

Her parents said it was her choice, but she had to go back to school somewhere to get a degree. She still would have to figure out something she could do. After taking an aptitude test, Marianne discovered, to no surprise, that her primary strength was music. However, she also found out that her secondary strength was human services because she loves people. And the third area of aptitude was outdoor work. She attributes the outdoor work to helping her dad in the garden while growing up. So she put the first two attributes together and started studying speech pathology at Penn State.

Eventually, she transferred to Duquesne University in Pittsburgh. The administrator recommended she finish her music degree since she had already accumulated so many credits.

Although she felt like music was dead to her, Marianne started to sing again with a new voice teacher who lovingly said to her, "If you don't sing, it will haunt you for the rest of your life."

Marianne listened and has never looked back.

After finishing her degree, she worked for three years in the Pittsburgh Opera's Young Artist program. She then went to the Metropolitan Opera House to sing small roles for five years.

Marianne learned that although you have set backs, and things don't look the way you thought they would, you have to continue to fight and figure out how to make "them" play with you.

Manhattan School of Music was the wrong choice for Marianne. She was doing what everyone else wanted her to do. Her vocal coaches were always telling her, "You're going to study. You're going to do a solo. You're going to go to the Manhattan School of Music." But it's not enough to be correct, or rational, or even inspired. When giving advice, influential people must understand what their listener is thinking and feeling, both in their mind and their heart.

You can have the best message or intentions in the world, but the person on the receiving end will always understand it through their perception of reality. I've learned that people don't see the world as it really is; they see it as they perceive it. The same is true with the words that you say to people. They don't hear what you really say; they hear what they perceive you said.

When we speak to others, we may choose positive and encouraging messages such as "you are smart," "you will be successful," "you are such a blessing to us," or "I am happy to have you here." These messages will uplift them.

At times, we may also be called upon to give advice or criticism, and here is where we need to carefully choose our words. Often the words we choose can cause damage, or have a negative influence, that will last for years.

People's words, while meant well, have caused damage in my life and in the lives of other women. Make sure your words encourage others instead of tearing them down.

Lipstick Lessons

Your words have their own energy; use them to build up rather than tear down.

Guard your heart and do not let those with negative words into your inner circle.

As a woman of influence you must **choose your words carefully.**

When asked for your advice, **choose positive and encouraging messages.**

The way you talk to people shapes your relationships and your relationships shape your life.

Chapter 7

Change the Script

"It's not who you are that holds you back, it's who you think you're not." - Author Unknown

The power of other people's words shapes your life and carries over into your physical and emotional health. If you've always heard positive words, your internal voice may be fairly easy on you. However, if you, like most people, have heard a lot of negative words, your internal critic may be playing those critical and condemning words over and over in your head.

Words, whether external or internal, shape your world. If you're having a challenge in your life, whether they be health, finances, personal, or business, examine the phrasing you hear in your head. Are they supporting or hindering your progress? At times, we internalize the criticism we hear from others, but our internal voice may just as likely offer us the answers. The key is to not only listen to what you are telling yourself, but to also examine the messages you are communicating.

Everyone knows that your internal dialogue impacts how you feel, but did you know it can also determine what you believe to be true and achieve? Make sure you are not listening to the wrong message.

The first step toward managing your self-talk is becoming more aware of it. For example, when you make a mistake, do you hear a voice in your head saying, "How could I have been so stupid?" When you ask such questions to yourself, your subconscious will look for answers as to why you are so stupid. If you think, "Someday I want to be rich," your brain will explore how you can become rich someday, in the future, not now.

What do you say when you talk to yourself? If you are critical and condemning, it is difficult to move forward in a spirit of success. Do you keep thinking and telling yourself that you cannot do something, that you are lazy, lack inner strength, or that you are going to fail? Often, we repeat negative statements in our minds, without even being aware of what they are doing.

Your subconscious mind accepts what you say internally as truth, and eventually attracts corresponding events and situations into your life that align to those messages, regardless of whether they are good or bad.

So how do you choose positive statements?

The Voice of Truth

After the transgression that ended my previous career (in case you missed the Introduction), I ran three to five miles every day. While I plodded through those long miles, I listened to my Walkman™ radio. One day the song, "Voice of Truth" blasted into my ears.

I stopped plodding to pay attention to the lyrics.

> *But the giant's calling*
> *Out my name*
> *And he laughs at me*
> *Reminding me of all the times*
> *I've tried before and failed.*
> *The giant keeps on telling me*
> *Time and time again,*
> *"Boy you'll never win!"*
> *"You'll never win."*
>
> *But the voice of truth*
> *Tells me a different story,*
> *The voice of truth says,*

> *"Do not be afraid!"*
> *The voice of truth says,*
> *"This is for my glory."*
> *Out of all the voices*
> *Calling out to me*
> *I will choose to listen*
> *And believe the voice of truth.*

As I listened, tears came to my eyes. I knew the lyrics were true. Furthermore, the scripts running through my head—the ones telling me what a failure I was, how I wouldn't amount to anything, how bad I was—were lies.

I knew I had to change the script in my head. I had to find some way to focus on the positive things I had accomplished—the truth about who I am as a person, not what others were saying about me.

You Are Your Words

The words you speak inside your head become you—and you become the words you use.

Changing the script and developing a positive voice in your head, is one of the most powerful success strategies there is. When you use powerful, positive thinking techniques, visualizations, and positive affirmations, it is possible to achieve whatever you want. As women, whether your are a stay-at-home mom or a business professional, you can use these techniques to develop personal power or gain a competitive edge.

When I first became a speaker for the public seminar company, I began to listen to the CDs that we sold during the training sessions. The very first one I listened to was Brian Tracy's *The Psychology of Achievement;* it literally changed my life!

It was the first time I heard the message of positive affirmations. Prior to that, in the Christian arena, I knew we were supposed to quote scripture over our lives, but I didn't know that we could create our own powerful statements. Tracy encourages people to say, in front of a mirror, statements such as, "I like myself" and "I feel terrific."

At first, I felt silly saying these statements out loud, but, as I started grabbing hold of the concept, I knew they could change my life.

I learned that affirmations are positive statements that describe a desired situation. Because they are repeated, they impress the subconscious mind and trigger it into positive action. In order to ensure the effectiveness of the affirmations, they have to be repeated with attention, conviction, interest, and desire.

One of the women I met at the trainer certification for the public seminar company sky-rocketed to the top in her customer satisfaction and sales. I asked her what she was doing differently from the rest of us. I learned that she had recorded her own CD of positive affirmations and listened to it before each seminar day. She said those words changed her reality

No Negative Thoughts Allowed

But simply saying positive affirmations in the morning is not enough. Understand that repeating a positive script for a few minutes in the morning, and then thinking negatively the rest of the day, defuses the effects of the positive words. You have to refuse to think negative thoughts, if you want to achieve positive results.

The solution is to catch that internal critic when it tries to take over, and stop it in its tracks before it has had a chance to believe its words. When you make a mistake or feel like you've failed, instead of reminding yourself how stupid you are, think instead, "What can I do next to fix this?" Now you're working on the solution.

Do not deny any realities of your failure; you can analyze the situation if you need to, cry if you want to, but move on as quickly as possible.

Choose positive words that describe what you really want. It's important to remember that every topic has two sides—that which you desire and that which you wish to avoid. Be careful to say the words describing what you want, and not what you are trying to avoid. For example, if you want to lose weight, instead of saying, "I don't want to be fat," say to yourself, "I am trim and fit." Focus your attention on what you want, not what you don't want, and be sure that your script focuses on the positive.

Always write your affirmation scripts in the present tense, not the future tense. Saying, "I *will* be rich," means that you intend to be rich one day, in the indefinite future, but not now. It is more effective to say—and feel and believe—"I am rich now." Once you say this, your subconscious mind will work overtime to make it happen now, in the present.

My pastor often says, "Elevate your thinking, and elevate your life!" The power of a positive script can help you transform your life. By stating what you want to be true in your life, you mentally and emotionally see and feel it as true, regardless of your current circumstances. The result? You will attract what you seek into your life.

We relocated to Dallas in 2005. My husband, Mark, started over in a brand new career. I began working on my Masters Degree and trying to become known as a national trainer and speaker. At the time, our income was about 25% of what we had been accustomed to.

It was a very scary time. There would be nights when I would wake from a sound sleep, covered in sweat, my heart racing, and the thought "How are we going to pay the bills?" running through my head. There was so much fear, that it was very difficult to think of anything positive.

But in the morning with the light of day, I was always able to come back to a voice of reason in my head that would assure me that everything was going to be alright. We would figure this out.

It has, however, taken me years to get over the night frights. Up until 2009, I struggled with them regularly. Then one day my friend, Elyse, told me that I needed to focus my thoughts on the positive things I wanted to bring into my life—and not the negative. She explained that when I focused on the negative, it was as if I was marching right towards them and causing them to become real.

Choosing to change your scripts to only positive thoughts is a practice. It requires that you have a certain mental attitude. When you have a positive thinking mindset, you will automatically generate positive thoughts. These thoughts will be reinforced when you recite positive affirmations.

Realize that this process doesn't happen overnight. It takes time to retrain old habits. Believe me, it took me many months of determined effort to shut off the negative scripts in my head, and replace them with those that contributed to my success.

Once you get into the habit of choosing a positive script, you will start to see happiness, good health, success, and positive outcomes in just about every situation and event. You will begin to trust and know that, when presented with awesome opportunities, you will make the right choices. You simply have to change your mindset, and throw out the old scripts.

Lipstick Lessons

Your self-talk impacts how you feel and determines what you believe.

The words you are speaking inside your head become you, and you become the words you speak.

Go ahead and stand in front of a mirror and **say, "I like myself" and "I feel terrific."**

If you want to achieve positive results, **refuse to think negative thoughts.**

Elevate your thinking and elevate your life.

Chapter 8

God Colored Outside the Lines. So Can You

"When you come to a roadblock, take a detour."
  – Barbara Bush

As women, we have been taught our entire life to color in between the lines, keep it pretty, and never make a mess.

In life, and in business, sometimes the best answer, and the most productive response, may be outside the lines.

My first memory of not staying inside the lines was in kindergarten. Because I have a September birthday, I started kindergarten when I was four years old. Since I was younger than the rest of my classmates; I sought ways to keep up with them.

I remember one particular assignment that always caused trouble for me. You know those maze activities we got as kids, where we had a mouse at one end of the maze and a block of cheese at the other? It was our job to get the mouse to the cheese through a twisted myriad of paths that would inevitably stop at a dead end.

To me, that just didn't make sense. Here is the mouse, there is the cheese. Draw a straight line between the two. Done!

The maze activities always came before snack break and recess. I would repeatedly be called in from recess to re-do my maze activity. The nuns insisted that I had to stay inside the lines to get the mouse to the cheese.

I remember looking at them so perplexed, and trying to explain to them what a complete waste of time that was. I would show them, "Here's the mouse. There's the cheese When I draw a straight line, that's the quickest way for him to get his snack." Unlike me, who continually missed our snack of crackers and Kool-aid because I was inside re-doing an assignment the "right way."

The nuns never did see it my way. No matter how persuasive I may have been at four years old, with my pixie hair cut and big brown eyes, they just weren't buying my argument.

It's not that I was looking for the easy way out, I just couldn't figure out why they wanted to make it so complicated. I was trying to be efficient and make the best use of my time. It seemed quite elementary to me.

I've found that same challenge through most of my life. It is comical to me that I can never turn off the impulse to cut through the maze and draw a straight line to my target.

I travel almost weekly, so I have an opportunity to see many silly things, especially in the hospitality industry.

For example, at a hotel recently, I watched in amazement as customers tried to navigate the existing system to get their "cooked to order" breakfast. The trays were at one end, silverware all the way across the room. Walk another 30 feet to get your coffee or juice, and back around for fruit.

I couldn't help but think to myself—if you moved this station to the left, brought these products over here, coffee and juices here, move the silverware to the front of the line. Done! I've just cut your serve time in half.

Letting Go of Heirlooms

In every situation you enter, you have a choice. You can choose to keep doing it the way it's always been done, or you can determine that there is a better way to do it.

I teach in my seminars that many of us hang onto heirlooms simply because that is the way we were taught it's supposed to be done. One of my favorite stories I tell in class is of a newlywed couple that is preparing their Christmas dinner. The young wife was getting ready to cook the ham. As she was about to put the large ham in the oven to begin baking, she started to cut off the ends of the ham.

Her husband stopped her saying, "Wait! That is my favorite part of the ham. Why are you cutting off the ends?"

Puzzled, the young wife responded, "Because that's the way my mother taught me to do it."

The husband decided to call his mother-in-law to find the reason for cutting off the best part of the ham. "Mom," he asked, "Why do we cut off the ends of the ham before baking it?"

"Well, that's how my mother taught me to do it, and it's the way I've always done it," replied the mother.

Well, now the husband really wanted to get to the bottom of the mystery, so he made one more call, this time to grandma. "Grandma," he asked, "Why is it necessary to cut off the ends of the ham before we bake it?"

"Well, honey," grandma replied, "I never had a pan big enough to fit the entire ham, so I cut off the ends to make it fit the pan."

And so it goes, from generation to generation, until someone asks "Why?"

The challenge, for many of us, is that we do not realize we have a choice.

If You Keep Doing What You've Always Done . . .

I can tell you that I was 42 years old before I realized I had a choice. After my transgression, I was working with a counselor in Dallas, and he looked at me and said, "One of the benefits of being a grown up is that you have a choice."

I looked at him not understanding what he was saying to me. I replied, "No, I don't. All my choices are made for me."

The counselor patiently told me, "You can choose anything you want. There is a consequence for each of your choices, but you do have a choice."

It took me nearly eight years to grasp that concept.

As women, we are so conditioned to stay within the lines:

"Sit still with your ankles crossed."

"Don't wrinkle your skirt."

"Don't make too much noise."

"Don't be pushy."

"If you act that way, people are going to think you are rude."

"Don't speak up."

"Men don't like women who are competitive."

"Don't put your lipstick on in public—it's unprofessional."

But you know the old saying, "If you keep doing what you've always done, you'll keep getting what you've always gotten."

So the question is, "Are you happy with the results you're getting?" Maybe it's time to make some choices that are best for you.

It is a tragedy to believe or behave as if you have no choices. After all, in every situation you have three choices: accept, change, or leave. You can accept the situation and go with the flow. Change the situation, your response, or your options. Or, you can simply walk away. The last one is the most difficult for women who feel they need to fix something. It goes against our motherly nature to simple leave it alone.

Make Unconventional Choices

My advice? Make unconventional choices. You don't have to go the way of average. What is right for your best friend may not be right for you. It's OK to be different. We, as women, can encourage each other on our different journeys.

People will say, "You can't do it your way. You have to do it the way it's always been done." These comments are nothing more than their efforts to make you fit into what they think you should be.

For instance, people told Mary Kay that she couldn't start a successful cosmetics company—and look what she did!

Mary Kay was successful in her sales career, and her supervisors praised her work, but they never increased her earnings.

She left the company after a man, whom she trained, was given a more important job than her.

Mary Kay said she learned from this experience. It taught her that men did not believe a woman could succeed in business.

Mary Kay decided to prove the men wrong. She paid five hundred dollars for the legal rights to a line of skin care products and started her own company. Success came quickly, and now Mary Kay Cosmetics is the largest direct seller of skin care products in the United States.

Mary Kay had a clear plan and vision. What about you? Where can you begin? Take charge of your education. I don't mean in the formal sense. What are you doing to improve who you are? What is the last book you read that enhanced your skills and knowledge? If you can't remember, you are like the majority of people in our culture. Statistics show that 73 percent of high school graduates never read another book after graduating from high school. For college graduates, that number falls to 47 percent. If you want to expand your knowledge and skills, choose to be different. Take charge of your education.

We cannot wait for others to equip us for success. We need to take responsibility to get the information and skills that we need.

Owe My Soul to the Company Store

There are plenty of opportunities to learn and practice new skills. If you choose to be a stay-at-home mom, remain involved through education and participation in professional associations. Choose one afternoon a week to do volunteer work in your field of interest; this will allow you to stay current with network connections, technology, and trends.

If you are a business woman, choose not to make work your life. Sometimes we choose to work too many hours; worse, sometimes others will try to make that choice for you. You owe your company an honest day's work for an honest day's pay. You owe your company a reasonable amount of overtime, always without complaint, but you don't owe your company your soul.

During one especially busy time at work, I was told a story of how a famous evangelist had put his children into a boarding school, so he could follow the "Call of God in his life." Confused, I listened to the story, wondering if I was being asked to send my children away. I knew for certain that I was being asked to make a complete sacrifice of my family and personal time to meet the needs of the organization.

But your family is your most important responsibility. Do not let others tell you to abandon those closest to you. Make a conscious choice to never cancel plans with your children because of a workplace request, unless your job is on the line. Even then, think twice. The further you let your boundaries be pushed, the more will be expected from you in the future.

I remember one particular conversation where it was explained to me that my responsibilities, at the organization, were too important for me to miss any Wednesday night functions. As a result, I would not be able to attend my youngest son's little league games that season. That was not acceptable because my son would only have a few seasons in his life. In contrast, the organization would survive long after my son grew out of little league.

Realize that employers will ask you to do what is best for them; it may not be what is best for you. They can ask, and you can choose to accept, change, or leave.

When others attempt to invalidate your choices, look at it as normal—but don't give in. Understand that when any "system" changes, whether it's a work or family system, it tends to want to maintain its status quo.

People don't want you to change because, if you change, they'll have to change too. It's easier for things to stay the way they've always been. The only way for them to keep things "normal" is to make you put your needs on the back burner. It doesn't mean that their motivation is coming from a place of malicious intent; it's simply their desire to keep the status quo.

The Gap ... The Risk

Choose your own goals. The problem many women encounter is we often allow others to choose for us, sidetracking us from our dreams and goals. You may have what it takes to be successful, but if you lose yourself in someone else's priorities or cultural expectations, it will be difficult to stay on course to eventually achieve your goals.

Choose to be bold! Choose to take risks. Don't worry about how you're going to get to your goals. Once you identify the gaps, you'll be able to identify the resources needed to fill them. Here is one thing I know, the gap between where you are and where you want to be, is the risk you haven't taken, yet.

When my boys were very young, they decided to host their own Olympic Games. One of the events involved swinging as high as they could, and then jumping off to see who could jump the farthest. In their desire to be the best, they kept swinging higher and jumping farther. On an award winning jump, my oldest son, Louis, hit the ground hard and broke his ankle.

He won the event, but ended up on crutches for a couple weeks.

Although it may seem foolish that Louis pushed himself so far that he ended up getting injured, it is an indication of his spirit. He has always been one to take on a challenge and go after the things he wants, even at the risk of failure or injury.

How many of us can say that?

Often times, we choose to stay in the box that we have created, or allow others to create one for us. We are afraid to push against the boundaries of that box, to take the risk, or make the changes we want or need in life.

However, the gap between where you are and where you want to be is the risk you haven't taken, yet.

As you go through life, it is much easier—and more comfortable—to conform to behaviors you see modeled around you, than it is to step out and go after what you want. I am convinced that taking charge of your life, taking risks that you know you need to take, requires more courage than most are willing to muster.

Louis graduated from Texas State with a degree in Accounting. Not an easy get. It took him a few years longer than most because, as he worked on his degree, he was also pursuing his passion—music. He and his brothers are members of a band and, for a couple months each year, they pile into a van to tour and promote their music across the country.

Others told him that he could not get a college degree while being a member of a touring band. Louis was unwilling to let others make that choice for him; he wouldn't be put into that box.

Of course, it's much safer inside the box. If you never take risks, you'll never face possible failure. Chances are good that you're going to make a mistake; you might get injured, and the end probably won't look exactly as you had pictured it. It's only when you take the risk to step outside the boundaries of the box that you will experience the amazing things life has to offer you.

When I was told that my job was too important, and I would have to miss Joe's baseball games, I didn't dispute that decision; for that season, I missed most of Joe's games. Although I was saddened and torn by my decision, I wasn't courageous enough to choose what was best for me and my family.

It remains one of the biggest regrets in my life. However, I now realize that each circumstance I have gone through has brought with it new opportunities to learn more about myself.

When we allow others to tell us what we can and cannot do, we limit how much we learn about ourselves, and what we really can—and should—be doing. Instead of listening to others, we have to listen to ourselves, achieve our goals, and strive, as best we can, to improve the lives of those around us.

Lipstick Lessons

Sometimes the most productive and best answer will be **outside the lines.**

In every situation you have three choices: **accept it, change it, or leave it.**

Never cancel plans with your children because of a workplace demand, unless your job is on the line. Even then, think twice.

The gap between where you are and where you want to be **is the risk you haven't taken.**

When you allow others to tell you what you can and cannot do, you limit what you learn about yourself and what you can and should be doing.

Chapter 9

The World Needs You!

"If you have knowledge, let others light their candles in it."
  - Margaret Fuller

One Sunday, our pastor had us stand up and repeat these words aloud, "The world needs me!" At first, it felt rather strange and a bit like bragging to say it aloud, especially with all those people around. But as we repeated it, I started to get comfortable with the message. It has now become part of my daily mantra, with a twist, "The world needs you; it needs your sizzle!"

One of the most exciting aspects of sizzle is that we all have it. It's the reason you were born; the part of you that was created to make you unique. Most people have a hard time defining their sizzle, but they have it nonetheless.

The best way to determine your sizzle is to start making a difference in other people's lives. When you cultivate a compassion for others, it creates in you a true sense of authenticity.

If you truly embrace your sizzle, and focus on giving it as a gift to other people, nothing can stop you. People will want to be with you and around you. It will be easy for you to stand up and say, "The world needs me!"

A key component of sizzle is to become aware of your own value. Don't get stuck in comparing yourself with others. There will always be someone who is richer, prettier, and smarter than you are. And I know from talking to hundreds of women, that everyone has an area of doubt, insecurity, or need in their life.

Each one of us has value in this world; we have something to contribute, and our own set of capabilities. It is also important to recognize that each of us has our own journey to success, and it doesn't help us to compare our journey to someone else's achievements.

Rather than compare, we should focus on our sizzle and how we can help each other.

Circle of Success

My dad taught me that there is a Circle of Success. To be successful, make the people around you successful.

The world needs you to bring your sizzle and commit to a full day of giving from your heart. If it seems overwhelming, then practice the "Just for today..." technique. Say to yourself, "Just for today, I am going to commit to sharing my sizzle with the people around me."

A few years ago, I started wearing a rhinestone "Texas" pin. I wear it when I speak and travel. On practically every trip, someone will stop to talk with me about an old college roommate who lives in Texas, or a family member who served in the military and was stationed here.

Often times, I'll hear, "My mom would love that pin." When I hear this, I take the pin off my jacket, hand it to the person and say, "Give it to her. I hope she enjoys it." After all, it's easy enough to find another rhinestone "Texas" pin in Texas. I can always get another, but my act of giving will be remembered for a long time.

It's only a 30-second moment of sizzle, but when you start adding those up, you realize how much value you can bring to the people you encounter every day.

Look for women who need your sizzle. Choose to be a mentor. Look for people who you can align yourself with to create their success and yours as well.

One day, we were sitting in a School Board meeting discussing the pressing need to get our private school accredited. Different leaders had tried for 20 years to accomplish this task, and none had been able to achieve accreditation status.

In the meeting, the discussion turned to who was going to be given the task of making sure accreditation happened this time around. I avoided eye contact as I felt everyone's attention turn toward me. They chose to give me the responsibility.

I remember the sinking feeling I had when they assigned the task to me. My job responsibilities were already overwhelming, and now I had a whole other issue to deal with. In the end, the successful process of getting our school accredited turned out to be one of the most challenging and rewarding things I have done.

My best friend, Gay, has a tremendous amount of sizzle. She is a strategic thinker, organized, and able to stay focused on the task at hand.

We met for breakfast early in the accreditation-seeking process to figure out what needed done, who we needed to recruit to help, and what pitfalls we might encounter along the way. We determined that we needed to align ourselves with other people who had sizzle!

The World Needs You!

Three years later, and with the assistance of 65 staff members and volunteers, we sat in the library and heard that we were awarded accreditation.

My favorite memory of the accreditation process was when we were down to just a few weeks before the site visit. I was at the point where I was totally overwhelmed. I sat in our weekly meeting with the organization's leadership team, and shared with them the items that still needed to be done before the site visit. I was pleased and delighted when these leaders, who were not directly involved with the process, asked how they could help.

Each one of them used their sizzle to help achieve something that no one before us had been able to do. When I explained the things I needed help with, these strong, creative, and giving women didn't bat an eye; they simply chose an element that they knew they could help with. Not only did we accomplish our goals, we so wowed the site visit team, they had no choice but to grant us accreditation.

Be careful to avoid those who are not willing to share their sizzle with you. There are people who believe that there is not enough success for everyone. These individuals may see you as a competitor or opponent, rather than an ally or confidant. Ultimately, alignment with this type of person will slow you down, and cause you to shrink instead of grow. Avoid them, and do not allow them into your inner circle.

I recently had the opportunity to see this first hand. Looking back, I should have handled the situation differently. I won't make the same mistake again.

As a Business Gardener, I host live Bust Out™ events across the country to help people grow their business. At an event in Southern California, we had one participant who did not understand the Circle of Success concept at all!

When I met her Friday night at the VIP reception, she seemed nice enough as a person, but she was one of those people who was an incessant name dropper. Most of her conversation consisted of, "Do you know 'Big Name Speaker #1'? I went to their event... blah, blah, blah." And then five minutes later, "Do you know 'Big Name Speaker #2'? He asked me to work with him on this project... blah, blah, blah."

All evening, it was a non-stop litany of people she knew. I began to ask myself, "If you've done such big things, why are you here?"

At breakfast the next morning, she pulled me aside and said she had expected something totally different from the weekend. She thought there would be 200 people present and she had just come for the networking. Of course, she could have asked me at any point how many people were registered; it wasn't a secret. For these Bust Out™ events, we purposely keep the attendance below 25. This allows everyone a chance to discuss their business challenges and get real answers for their concerns. She told me she would sit in on some of the sessions, but couldn't afford to give her entire weekend to the event.

Because the Bust Out™ events are so intense, it works best when participants and presenters are there for all the sessions. It is too small of a format for people to jump in and out of, and her spirit was not aligned with the spirit of the weekend. From the start, these events have been one of giving, and she seemed to be in the habit of taking.

We started the first year with no registration fee, and the cost of admission was what you could bring to help others. We now bring in expert speakers on specific topics. It has been wildly successful for most of the participants. They get the information and connections they need to start taking their business to new levels.

However, some participants are just bad seeds, and this woman in particular sticks out in my memory. One of our very nice male participants sat next to her during the general sessions. As she continued to name drop the entire day, he leaned over and asked her a question about a specific topic, as well as a recommendation for a mentor in that area. She looked at him point-blank and said, "Look Brian, you're going to have to pay the same $15,000 I did to get that information."

Unfortunately, I didn't hear about the conversation until the next day. I was hurt for Brian, and disappointed in the woman's behavior. Yes, you have to be willing to invest in yourself in order for others to be willing to invest in you, but you also have to be willing to practice the Circle of Success and help those around you be successful!

I learned a valuable leadership lesson that weekend. When she pulled me aside at breakfast I should have explained the spirit of the weekend to her once again, and offered her a choice to either come on board and commit to sharing her knowledge with the other participants, or take a refund and leave.

The world, or at least the participants of that Bust Out™ weekend, needed me to bring my leadership gifts.

Abundance Brings Abundance

The Circle of Success operates from a spirit of abundance, rather than lack. Some people are afraid to share their knowledge because they believe there is not enough to go around. Their attitude is, "If I tell you my secrets, you'll steal customers from me."

To approach life from a place of lack can only bring lack, even when you get what you think you need. On the other hand, when you come from the spirit of abundance, you attract even greater abundance.

As we operate in the spirit of abundance, we become a liberating and empowering force in the lives of people we interact with. We help them see, through our example, that they too can live with a spirit of abundance.

You already have a lot to be grateful for, even in the worst of times. Wherever you are, and whatever your circumstances, allow yourself to move away from feelings of scarcity and lack to the realization of abundance.

One of the best and easiest ways to create a mindset of abundance is to celebrate and appreciate what you already have. Appreciation for who you are and what you have, even when it seems far from your ideal, is more useful than a "poor me" attitude. Such an appreciation frees you to make changes and create success and abundance.

If you can't readily find things in your life to celebrate, turn your focus outward and find someone to help. Practice the Circle of Success with the next person you come in contact with. By planting seeds of encouragement and success in someone else's life, the universe will return these seeds as full-grown plants into your own life.

The world needs you. Create a natural flow of energy and abundance in the truest sense. Base your actions on cooperation, rather than competition. It is through your gifts, what you have as a woman, that the spirit of abundance will be activated in the lives of those you touch ... as well as your own.

Lipstick Lessons

The world needs you!

Embrace your sizzle by giving it as a gift to others.

Practice the Circle of Success to be a success; make the people around you successful.

Create a mindset of abundance by focusing on those things you are grateful for.

When you operate with a spirit of abundance you **become an empowering force** in the lives of those around you.

Your Face Isn't Finished Until Your Lipstick is On

Chapter 10

Be Lovingly Consistent

"Perseverance is failing nineteen times and succeeding the twentieth." - Julie Andrews

In my years as a business coach, seminar leader, and speaker, I have been very fortunate to work with women who want to achieve both personal and professional goals. Their dreams and goals are inspiring, and it is my passion to positively contribute to their success.

Often I am asked a very important question, "What is the difference between the women who reach their goals versus the ones who don't?"

The difference usually boils down to one simple fact; those who succeed, take action. They just do it.

Just do it; three simple words that carry a tremendous amount of power. Nike® made this phrase famous, but it's not just a marketing slogan. All you need is to "just do it," and you will reach a critical tipping point where you go from talking and planning … to living it.

One thing I have learned is that successful women do things differently than those who struggle. "Just doing it" seems to be one of the major differences between achievers and those still looking forward to achievement. Successful women have more of what they want, are engaged in the career they want, and have the kinds of relationships they want. Those who don't, don't.

You've Got 30 Seconds

The first step towards success is being able to articulate what you truly want, both in your personal and professional life. Unfortunately, most of us can tell others what we don't want, but the majority of women have a difficult time clearly stating what they do want in life.

Make a list of different areas of your life, for example: career, finances, spirituality, family, health, education, etc. Grab a stopwatch and pick one of the categories, let's say career. In 30 seconds, write down something you want to have, something you want to be, and something you want to do in your career. Then move to the next item and give yourself another 30 seconds to write down a have, be, and do goal for that category, and so on.

Don't be surprised if you have a difficult time accomplishing this task. Most women do. The important thing is to begin to focus on identifying the things you know you want in each of those areas. You can go back and fill in the blanks later.

If you're still stuck, it is okay to think about what you don't want in each category. Once you have that concept in mind, change it to something you do want. After all, you attract what you focus on. Make sure your focus is on what you want in each category, not what you don't want.

Once you have your list, it is time to take action —easier said than done. Setting goals is one thing; achieving them is yet another. Too often we allow procrastination, conflicting priorities, or fear of the unknown stop us from moving forward. Repeatedly, I see women failing to get the results they hope for because they do not take the necessary actions.

The thing to understand is that no one ever succeeds on their own. When you see someone who is successful, no matter how they might tell the story, realize that there were countless people who aided them on their journey.

For you to reach your goals, you will need people to help you along. You cannot succeed, truly succeed, without others. So surround yourself with a strong network of like-minded people who will help you reach your goals.

My dad always taught me that you are only as strong as your network. As a woman, it is particularly important to strategically align yourself with others who will help you achieve your dreams.

If you've chosen to be a stay-at-home mom, be careful not to isolate yourself from women who are active in the marketplace. Purposefully get involved in activities outside of the home, at least for a couple hours a week. Volunteer at your church or another local non-profit. Always seek those who are more creative, more talented, more experienced, and more skilled than you. Choose not to be intimidated by them; instead, find out what they've done that has worked and do the same in your life. When you adopt and adapt their success strategies, you will start to see similar success in your life.

Show Me Your Friends ... I'll Show You Your Future

When you look at your friends, who do you see? Chances are you see people who look much like you. It's often said that people are a reflection of their five closest friends. You'll see this in behaviors, values, income levels, and so on. For instance, if I take the average of your five closest friends' income, I'll probably arrive at a number that is scarily close to yours.

To put it simply, if you want to find success beyond what you're able to find right now, you may have to re-evaluate your circle of friends. A good circle of friends is supportive and reinforces your best attributes. If you don't like what you see, it likely means you're growing as a person in a direction away from some of your friends—and that's fine.

I'm not saying to ditch your friends, but my belief is that people change and grow over time. That growth is often reflected in who you choose to spend your time with. If you feel like you cannot change your inner circle of friends, be all that more determined to make healthy network relationships with women who are outside of your immediate circle. Intentionally seek out others who better reflect your values, and work on establishing a relationship with them.

Surround yourself with people who can help you achieve your goals. It comes naturally for most women to collaborate, so use that gift to help you achieve your dreams and goals. The more you surround yourself with women who can complement what you are trying to achieve, the more chance for success you will have.

I had a young woman in my seminar recently who had chosen a very specific career and family path. She stayed after class to talk with me, and explained that she had just turned 27. On her birthday, she received her latest promotion which put her income over the $100,000 mark. She said that when she graduated from college, her plan was to go on to get her MBA, make $100K by the time she was 30, and then meet someone, get married ,and have a family. So far, she was right on track with her goals.

She also said that, at times, it was lonely for her because many of her friends from high school and college had already married and were having children. She has had to be strategic about seeking relationships with other business women, and she often chooses those who are older than her to stay on track with her goals.

She was determined to "just do it" and developed a plan around her goals.

I admit that it's pretty scary to take a plunge into something like "just do it" implies. That is why you must surround yourself with women who are going in the same direction as you and who will help you get rid of the excuses.

We all have excuses; they sound something like this:

"I don't have enough money."

"I don't have enough time."

"I don't know the right women."
"I don't know where to start."
"I don't know how."
"I'll do it later."

Instead of whining, crying, or complaining when you're discouraged, choose to funnel that energy into focus and action. Yes, it's risky, and it might get you in trouble. You might even fail, but if you get caught up in the "what if's", you will never take the steps to achieve what you want.

To ensure that you step past excuses, it may help you to get an accountability partner who will help keep you on track to reach your goals.

When my family and I moved to Dallas, one of the things I missed the most was the 5:00 a.m. knock on my front door from my friend Gay. She was diligent to show up three mornings a week, so that we could walk our three miles. After moving, I found it was much harder for me to get up and exercise without someone there to hold me accountable.

Without someone to hold us accountable, we often find excuses for not doing what needs to be done. Sometimes, our accountability partner can be our friend, but often we have to reach out to a mentor or coach to ensure that we stay on track with our goals.

Did He Just Call Me Fat?

As a professional speaker and trainer, I am in airports most weeks, and I see all kinds of people. I have always been a people watcher, and an airport is a great place to practice my pastime. One thing I noticed about road warriors (frequent fliers) is, for the most part, they are either really fit or really out of shape.

When I turned 50 (or as I like to say, forty-ten) I decided it was time to be in the fit and in-shape category. So I gave myself the birthday present of greater dedication to my health and fitness.

My problem is not that I fail to *choose* to exercise every day; most days it never crosses my mind. I don't make a decision not to exercise, I simply fail to notice that I haven't exercised until the day has past.

So when Robert offered to assist as my personal coach, I jumped on the offer.

He told me to weigh and measure myself, and we'd get started. As a woman, I bet there aren't many people you're willing to share your weight and measurements with, unless you are one of the those who are blessed with a perfect body and metabolism. I'm not so fortunate, but I figured, "what the heck, let's do this." After all, I've been battling with my weight since I was 3 years old. If I didn't address things now, they weren't going to get better by themselves.

After the first week, I had gained 4 pounds—not exactly the results I was looking for. During our phone appointment, I said to Robert, "I just don't know if I can do this."

At that point, the tiger in him came out, and Robert became someone I really didn't like. He said, "When you walk on stage, people see a chubby woman."

Inside I said, "Whimper, whimper."

He continued, "I want you to join Weight Watchers and get to a meeting this week."

I responded, "But Robert, that's where the fat people go."

"Well Monica, at 5'3" and 155 pounds ...."

To myself I announced, "I think he just called me fat!"

One month later I'd dropped 10 pounds. I was on the treadmill at least 5 days a week, and even though I still didn't like Robert, I respected his toughness with me.

Now I have the Robert Rule for eating. It goes like this, "If I had to tell Robert I ate this, how would I feel?" As a result, I haven't had a Quarter Pounder with cheese in quite awhile. My goal is to drop another 20 pounds, get my blood pressure under control, and run a 5K race.

If you are serious about your business and personal goals, an accountability partner will help you stay on track. The reality is that any goal worth having takes time, hard work, and determination, and the results never come as quickly as we want them to. Begin working with an accountability partner and you may get results sooner than you think.

The Good Life Formula

Wanting to enjoy a good life is common. We all want good health, positive relationships, fulfilling careers, and enough money to live comfortably. But what are we willing to do to achieve these milestones?

You didn't get to where you are today without taking some sort of action, so it makes sense if you have a mental vision of where you would like to be in the future. The problem with most women is, even though they may have the knowledge to do a particular thing, they fail to put the necessary action behind that knowledge.

One of the things I teach in my seminars is the concept, Information ≠ Transformation. We often hear that "knowledge is power," but knowledge is useless if there is not some accompanying action. Knowledge that is not put into action remains "inside" information and provides no "outside" benefits. It's completely wasted.

To accomplish results, we must couple our knowledge with the necessary action. The formula for achieving results is: Information + Application = Transformation. If you apply action to your knowledge, it will have a tremendous impact on your life.

The smallest of actions, even the ones that seem trivial and insignificant, can lead to great success. So why is it that most women find it difficult to put the necessary action behind their knowledge?

It comes back to forward motion; just get moving! Once you've taken the first step, the next steps are easier. Information and knowledge is fundamental, but, in the end, taking action is essential.

If you want to be successful, you must start at the beginning. Most beginnings are small, and appear trivial and insignificant, but they are extremely important. It's not only the right beginning that is important; it's beginning in the first place. It's about applying that powerful little phrase, "Just Do It!"

Lipstick Lessons

The difference between women who reach their dreams versus the ones who don't comes down to **taking action.**

Instead of telling us what you *don't* want, grab your stopwatch and set your 30 second goals of **what you do want**.

Strategically align yourself with others who will help you achieve your dreams.

Funnel your fears into focus and action.

An accountability partner will help you get results.

**Information + Application
= Transformation**

Apply action to your knowledge to bring impact to your life.

Conclusion

"Learn as much as you can about as much as you can."
– Monica Cornetti

In these pages, I have laid out a message of mistakes, failures, falling down and learning how to get back up again.

Most of us grew up with the Cinderella fantasy of how our life would turn out: a handsome Prince Charming will gallop in on a massive white horse, pause, reach down with one arm to easily lift us up. Together we will ride off into the happily ever after.

But things rarely go as planned. I don't know about you, but I have yet to have Cinderella's life. Our life, family and career are complex and seldom a fairy tale.

As you walk along your journey of life, you will enjoy wins and encounter failures. No matter who we are, good things as well as bad are part of the voyage.

A few years ago, we took a family vacation to the Hawaiian islands of Oahu and Kauai. We had budgeted our money and planned our trip in great detail, attempting to include at least one thing that each person really wanted to do in paradise.

When we arrived at our condo on Kauai, we were thrilled to discover that it was beautifully situated right at the edge of a cliff overlooking a hidden beach. We couldn't have asked for a more beautiful place to spend four days of sun and surf.

For our first full day, we rented scooters to explore the island. I was a little shaky on my test run in the parking lot, but felt confident that I could handle the machine once I got used to it. The man who rented us the bikes drew a map of hidden waterfalls that only the locals knew of, and we set out ready to have a great adventure.

After much searching, we found the first waterfall; it was truly amazing. There was a huge tree with a rope attached. You could swing out over the falls, and then drop 50 feet or so into the water below. The boys were brave enough to not only take the swing, but to also leap from the cliffs above.

As for me, I sat on the rocks at the top of the falls and watched the fun my boys were having.

Conclusion

When they were done with the water, we set out for more exploring. We headed up a narrow, winding, mountain road in search of the next waterfall.

I was surprised at the number of cars driving in both directions. The drivers were impatient with us because the scooters only go about 35 to 40 mph and it's tough to get around them on a narrow road. Cars would honk occasionally, and it was unnerving. I had a hard time understanding how anyone could be in such a hurry while in paradise.

As I approached a bend in the road, I must have been too close to the center line. As the car coming in the opposite direction rounded the bend, I got really spooked, panicked, and lost control of the scooter.

That is the last thing I remember until I heard the voice of the EMT officer asking me if I knew my name and where I was. By this time, I was in an ambulance on my way to the hospital. Evidently I had run off the road, hit a sign, and was thrown head first into the grass and gravel.

My oldest son, Lou, had been behind me. He froze on his scooter and could only stare at me. He couldn't even get off his scooter to check on me because he was certain I was dead.

My husband, Mark, had seen the entire incident in his rear view mirror. He turned around to get back to me. When he rolled me over, my face was covered in blood and dirt, and the gravel had matted my hair and covered my clothes. My arm looked like it was detached and was just lying next to my body.

At the hospital, we learned that I had a concussion, and had sustained a broken and dislocated left shoulder. I had cuts and bruises all over my face and most of my body. I looked like I had been on the losing end of a bad bar fight. After hours of CT scans and x-rays, they stabilized my shoulder and told me that I would have to see an orthopedic surgeon once I got home.

I had never experienced anything like that in my life. The pain in both my head and arm was terrible. I was nauseous from the pain, and the medication made it worse. It was a miracle that I was even alive.

Victims are Helpless

For the next four days in Hawaii, I spent most of my time lying on a lawn chair on a grassy area that overlooked the ocean. As I listened to the pattern of waves crashing below, I remembered what I heard a speaker once say about crises in our life. He said that you can expect crises to come in your life just like the waves come in with the ocean—usually three small waves, and then one big CRASH!

Conclusion

Bad things happen to good people every day; you can count on it. When these times come, it's important that we do not adopt a victim mentality. Victims are helpless. When we think like a victim, we believe that we have no control over the situations we encounter. The truth is, we may not be able to control what happens to us, but we can decide how we're going to react in each situation.

When we feel like a victim, we tend to not take action because we don't want to risk rejection or failure. When we are in a victim mentality, we don't see the range of choices we have, and we wallow in resentment. We feel helpless.

To remove that victim mentality, we have to accept the reality of the situation, and search for the best choice available within that reality. We must feel and believe that we deserve what we want, and begin to take responsibility for ourselves and our lives.

When I lost my job at the nonprofit, and all hopes of being a successful career woman were dashed, I sat on a couch in my darkened bedroom and cried for hours. I thought my life was in ruins.

My boys were not fully aware of what was going on, so I tried for months to keep up a brave face for them. Finally, I realized they deserved an explanation from me. I sat down with them one by one to explain what happened, the choices I had made, and the consequences we would now face as a family.

They were confused by my behavior, and outwardly they remained supportive. Inwardly though, I know they struggled with the dichotomy of the woman they always thought I was, and the woman who had failed so dreadfully.

The whole incident became a meaningful signal to redirect my life. Sometimes, a tragedy provides us with an opportunity to rid ourselves of our old reality, and begin anew. I had just experienced a huge setback, and now it was time to gather my inner strength. I had to figure out a new set of rules to live my life as a wife, mother, and professional business woman.

We've been learning rules all our lives. We have been told what we should and should not do. And there were, of course, consequences to breaking those rules.

Rules Were Made to be Broken

There's an old saying that rules were made to be broken, but I tend to think that rules are made by someone else; they may not apply to me and my life. Sure, rules are necessary for society to function, but not all rules are rational, or even reasonable. I tend to look at each set of rules and ask, "Are these helping us to solve the problem, or are they complicating the issue?"

Conclusion

Our family recently attended one of the very popular 3-D movies. Because we knew it would be a full house, we purchased our tickets beforehand on the Internet. When we arrived at the theater, we simply had to print the tickets out and avoided standing in the box office line, a line that stretched down the length of the sidewalk and around the side of the building.

We were excited as we stood at the front of the line because we knew we would be able to pick the best seats in the house. We had a brief discussion about the 3-D glasses, and concluded they would probably be handed out once the doors to the theater were opened.

As we watched the other moviegoers, arrive we noticed that they were each carrying a set of 3-D glasses. I asked one of them where they had gotten their glasses, and they told me they were given to them at the box office when they purchased their tickets.

I noticed a theater employee walking by, and explained that, since we had purchased our tickets online, we had not received our glasses. I asked where we could get them.

He replied, "You have to go stand in line at the box office."

I asked, "You mean the line that wraps around the building? The reason we bought our tickets online was so we wouldn't have to stand in line."

He simply replied, "That's the only place to get them, you'll have to go stand in line."

This was a classic example of a rule that needed to be broken.

I put a smile on my face, and suggested we find his manager to see if there was another solution to the problem, which of course there was.

The manager walked into the office, retrieved five sets of glasses, and handed them to me.

Although this is a light hearted example of a rule, think how much anger was created in that theater by people who didn't believe that rules could and should be broken. Instead of seeking another solution, they begrudgingly walked outside in the cold weather, and stood in line for 30 minutes to get their glasses. Their victim mentality caused them to believe they had no choice.

When bad things happen, whether big or small, we want to stay agile and solution focused.

When you think about being lovingly persistent, be sure that you are being persistent about solutions and not the problems. The rules will always be there. It is up to you to decide if they are the best answer to your current situation, or if you need to bend or break a rule in order to find a solution.

In the meantime, let me suggest another set of rules that will help you achieve your goals and live the life you want.

Lipstick Lessons

Reframe the way you look at things.

Always **maximize your strengths and minimize your weaknesses.**

Reflect on accomplishment, and allow those feelings of accomplishment to be the foundation of your growing self-confidence.

Educate yourself. Learn as much as you can about as much as you can. Identify the skills you'll need to achieve your goals.

Practice positive self-talk. Write a strong script of personal affirmations that will help encourage you to stay strong when you feel like quitting.

If you fear it, try it. Find the courage to start again when you fall down. We have all made mistakes, and I guarantee that we will make many more before we're done. Let's focus on finishing strong.

And finally, **WEAR LIPSTICK!** It feels great and draws people to your smile. Get yourself some lipstick. Every time you apply it, remember that in the rules of the women's success game, you should have fun and enjoy life's challenges. It is possible to live an empowered life of fulfillment and success... **in your shade and on your terms.**

You've enjoyed reading her insights . . .
Now, bring Monica to speak to your organization or at your event.

Monica Cornetti is a highly sought after speaker and trainer. Her emphasis is always on fun and learning as she delivers high-energy, high-content training, along with a plan for application in the real world

Her client list includes: The Association of Small Business Development Centers, The International Association of Administrative Professionals, Infinisource, Rockhurst University, National Seminars Group, Park University, CareerTrack, Fred Pryor Seminars, and The National Association for Community College Entrepreneurship.

Her passion centers around helping entrepreneurs take their business to the next level of success and significance.

She's a natural-born motivator, optimist and entertainer. Her presentations are inspirational, funny, and focused on helping her participants achieve results.

Monica is a published author, a top-notch speaker, a professional consultant and an accomplished leader known for being one of the best entrepreneurial training experts in the business. With loads of spunk and charm, her skills as a speaker have earned her Perfect 10 reviews from participants across the country.

You can find Monica's speaking schedule at EntrepreNowOnline.com

Connect with Monica

Monica interacts with her audiences and readers through many different media. She appreciates those who want to stay in the conversation with her, and regularly offers insights and other treasures to her network.

Of course, you're invited to her website: EntrepreNowOnline.com. Here you will discover everything Monica, including her blog, speaking calendar, the different resources she has available, and even sign up for her newsletter.

Or, feel free to email her at Monica@EntrepreNowOnline.com

Totally Awesome Training Audio CD

Enough Already! No more dry, boring lectures.

Liven up your training programs so that you can become a more dynamic trainer. These proven methods increase participation, engage your audience, and get genuine results!

Totally Awesome Training Activity Guide

This is the tool you need to bring dynamic and interactive solutions to all your speaking and training. With more than 50 fun, interactive, and practical exercises to choose from, you'll soon be on your way to delivering totally awesome training that gets results.

Go ahead, break the rules, and tear out this page.

CPSIA information can be obtained at www.ICGtesting.com
Printed in the USA
BVOW072059120912

299891BV00001B/10/P

9 780978 922917